Lions Led by Donkeys

Lions Led by Donkeys

How to Make the Real Economy Work

Stephen Hill, FCA

Duckworth

First published in 1992 by
Gerald Duckworth & Co. Ltd.
The Old Piano Factory
48 Hoxton Square, London, N1 6PB
Tel: 071 729 5986
Fax: 071 729 0015

A catalogue record for this book is available
from the British Library

ISBN 0 7156 2455 5

Typeset by Ray Davies
Printed in Great Britain by
Redwood Press Ltd, Melksham

Contents

Graphs, tables & inserts   6
Acknowledgements   7
Abbreviations   8
Introduction   11

Part 1: Theory

1. The Two Primary Factors of Production   14

2. The Natural Economic Cycles   19

3. The Third Factor in Production and Distribution   29

4. Property vs. Industry in the Market Economy   42

5. The Problems of Corrupt Data and Corrupt Attitudes   50

6. The Primary Cause of Inflation and Unemployment   61

7. The Importance of the Incidence of Taxation   72

8. The Necessity for Common Markets   87

Part 2: Practice

9. An Economic Portrait of the 1980s   98

10. Taking Stock in the 1990s   116

11. Blueprint for Britain's Target 2000   131

12. Political Postscript   152

13. Ecological Postscript   158

14. Ten Fundamental Principles of Economics   165

15. SWOT Analysis of UK plc   167

Select bibliography   170
Index   171

Graphs, Tables and Inserts

Graph 1: Business Cycles – World Trade in Manufactures and G7 Industrial Production 1970-93 21

Graph 2: Britain's Industrial Problem – UK Volume Share of World Trade in Manufactures 1970-93 48

Graph 3: Britain's Private Debt Problem – Personal Sector Income Gearing 1970-93 49

Graph 4: Britain's 1988 Error – Money and Lending 1984-92 51

Graph 5: The Inflation Boom – G7 Growth and Inflation 1970-93 63

Graph 6: UK, German and ERM Consumer Price Inflation 1979-91 67

Table 1: Britain's GDP and the Decline of Manufacturing 46

Table 2: Britain's 1991-92 Budget 74-5

Table 3: Britain's Property Values in 1987 76

Table 4: Britain's 1991-92 Budget Reformatted for the Incidence of Taxation on the Two Primary Factors of Production 84

Table 5: Britain's Commercial Property Lending, November 1991 117

Table 6: The 1982-83 Recovery in Britain 118

Table 7: Local Authorities: 1990 Current Account 126

Table 8: Proposed Budget Changes, 1993-94 140

Table 9: Comparison of 1991-92 Actual Budget with Target for 2000-01 150

Insert 1: 'Make Mother Earth Happy. Buy This Shirt' 18

Insert 2: Who Needs the Treasury Computer? – Part One 71

Insert 3: 'Some Things Never Change' 85

Insert 4: 'It's All a Question of Timing' 96

Insert 5: Who Needs the Treasury Computer? – Part Two 114

Insert 6: 'The People's Budget' of 1909 156

Acknowledgements

First, I am indebteded to the late Andrew MacLaren, a traditional Liberal economist of 'the old school', who was MP for the Burslem Division of Stoke-on-Trent (1922-1945), for his clear explanations of the economic issues which were fought over in the election campaigns of 1909-10.

Secondly, I am indebted to Eliot Janeway, resident of New York City, for his comments on many of the points raised and for the inspiration of his latest book *The Economics of Chaos: On Revitalizing the American Economy*. His involvement does not mean that he necessarily concurs with all the ideas and proposals discussed in this book.

My thanks also go to Colin Haycraft, who edited the text, to Capt. Francis Bruen, R.N. (Ret'd), Clive Phillips and Dan Van Der Vat for their many helpful suggestions.

The cartoon on the front cover is by Mahood of the *Daily Mail*.

Abbreviations

AALOBB	'All a Load of Bloody Bollocks', or A^2LOB^2
BES	Business Expansion Scheme
BOBO	'Burnt Out But Opulent', not to be confused with GIGO
CAP	The Common Agricultural Policy of the EC
Central Government	Departmental activities where a Minister is responsible to Parliament
CFCs	Chlorofluorocarbons
DNA	Dioxyribonucleic Acid
DTI	Department of Trade and Industry
EC	European Community, formerly the European Economic Community (EEC)
ECB	European Central Bank
ECU	European Currency Unit (equivalent to 77.5 pence)
EFTA	European Free Trade Area
EMU	European Monetary Union
ERM	Exchange Rate Mechanism
FT-SE 100	*Financial Times* – Stock Exchange 100 Companies (drawn from the top 110 UK quoted companies)
GATT	The General Agreement on Tariffs and Trade, signed in 1946
GDP	Gross Domestic Product
GEC	The General Electric Company plc
GIGO	'Garbage In, Garbage Out', not to be confused with BOBO
GNP	Gross National Product
G7	Group of Seven leading economic powers
HLT	Highly Leveraged Transaction
IBM	International Business Machines Corporation
ICI	Imperial Chemical Industries plc
IMF	International Monetary Fund
KKR	Kohlberg, Kravis & Roberts, an American MBO firm
LDCs	Lesser Developed Countries

Local Government/ Authorities	Public authorities with limited geographic scope to raise certain forms of taxation, including county, borough, district and parish councils
MBO	Management Buy-Out
M0	'Narrow Money'
M4	'Broad Money'
NEC	Nippon Electric Corporation of Japan
OECD	Organisation for Economic Co-operation and Development (comprising 24 member countries, including the G7)
OPEC	Organisation of Petroleum Exporting Countries
OTEC	Ocean Thermal Energy Conversion
PSBR	Public Sector Borrowing Requirement
S&Ls	American Savings & Loan Associations
SME	Small and Medium-Sized Enterprises (an EC acronym)
SWOT	Strengths, Weaknesses, Opportunities, Threats
TESS'	Take equity stake/securitisation
TIM	Transferable insured mortgage
TSB	Trustee Savings Bank plc
UK	United Kingdom
US	United States
USSR	The former Union of Soviet Socialist Republics
UV	Ultra-violet
VAT	Value Added Tax
WW1&2	World War One & Two

'Labour is the Father ... of wealth, as lands are the Mother.'

Sir William Petty (1623-1687),
author of *Lands and Hands*.

'This dictum [by Petty] put on their feet the two original
factors of production of later theorists.'

Joseph A. Schumpeter (1883-1950),
author of *Business Cycles*.

Introduction

The worldwide recession of the early 1990s has humbled many an economist, politician and banker. Most of them did not see it coming and continued to talk about a 'soft landing' well into 1991. When the recession was generally admitted to be an actuality and even a severe 'hard landing', they called the recovery too early in the spring of 1992. As 1992 wore on, it seemed that no one had a clear idea of how to get the world economy moving again.

In America President Bush threw the dollar to the wolves baying for cheap interest rates, in an effort to gain votes at home and export orders with low-priced goods, and to stimulate domestic investment with cheap money, which was what the British used to do in the 1960s and 1970s when things went wrong. In Europe, on the other hand, the Germans raised interest rates to suppress inflation and to cope with surging monetary expansion caused by the problems of unification with East Germany, which was ecologically and economically bankrupt. These problems were compounded by the absurd decision to put the worthless Ostmark on a partial parity with the Deutschemark, the world's strongest currency. Britain became divided about whether to follow the American or the German example. The Prime Minister and the Chancellor of the Exchequer determined to follow the Germans in the pursuit of sound money and maintained interest rates at over 6% p.a. above the official rate of inflation for many months. The official rate of inflation, however, did not take into account the deflation of asset values that was being experienced, so many of Britain's industrialists, bankers and economists argued that the Government should follow the Americans, and cut interest rates to stimulate demand and let the pound sterling float. On 16th September 1992, the foreign exchange markets took the decision for them and the pound was forced to float and leave the ERM, along with the Italian lira. 'Lions led by donkeys' was how General Max Hoffman of the German General Staff described the British Tommy and their generals in WWI. The year 1992 turned out to be a case of *déjà vu* as businesses, jobs and homes were mown down by the recession while the government sat and watched. The Chancellor even announced that the rising unemployment was 'a price well worth paying'.

The Japanese, on the other hand, had to wade in with a £46 billion boost in August to prevent their stock and real estate markets from suffering

11

meltdown. The Ministry of International Trade and Industry had only hesi-
tantly reduced interest rates to save their financial assets, although Japanese
industry was still growing in the first half-year and clocking up enormous
trade surpluses. In the summer of 1992 the French farmers and truckers did
what they know best and blocked the country's entire road and distribution
system with their tractors and trucks in pursuit of their own sectional interests.
The Italians, meanwhile, were forced to raise their bank rate to 16.5% in
September and put a state industry into bankruptcy with debts of over £3.5
billion, passing a decree to repudiate the state's obligations at the same time.
Canada, the last of the recognised Group of Seven economies, was reeling
with the effects of two of the world's biggest corporate insolvencies, caused
by a Toronto-based property developer's operations in America, Britain and
Canada running out of tenants and cash, and a major retailer going bust with
over C$ 6 billion debt, taken on as a result of a highly leveraged transaction.
And to cap it all, the G7 economies experienced the most volatile foreign
exchange rate gyrations seen since 1945, which nearly took the thirteen-year-
old ERM apart at the seams in September.

The world is awash with economic theories, statistics and information
which are updated quarterly, monthly and weekly. Markets are now global,
and prices are set every second for shares, debts, commodities, futures,
metals, bullion, crops, charters, energy and exchange or discount rates for
money instruments. The universities turn out more graduate economists every
year, who find employment with government agencies, bankers, brokers and
independent forecasters. These economists analyse more data and publish
more findings, opinions and advice than ever before. The 'man or woman on
the Clapham Omnibus' has a right to know and is entitled to ask: do these
experts know what they are doing? Do they, or some of them at least, know
what is going on? Is it possible to understand economics in the first place?
And if so, how is it that we suffer from the Economics of the Madhouse across
the world? Or have they overlooked something so fundamental that their
theories and calculations are based on false or mistaken premises?

This last question is the important one because, if this proves to be the
case, all is not lost and remedies may even be at hand. In an age which has
examined economics apparently from every conceivable angle, but has
formulated conflicting theories concerning monetary systems, taxation, finance, employment, prices, wages, rents, costs and distribution systems, each
supported by extensive and elaborate data and argument, it would be a relief
for the general public to be informed in simple terms that modern economics
is essentially flawed, that it was all a bad misunderstanding, that there was a

fundamental oversight all along, that a correction over a period of time, with retraining for those in positions of responsibility, is possible and necessary, so that the economy really could be managed more effectively in the future. What joyful news this would be for all those families and businesses struggling to make ends meet and seeking to enjoy life and prosper more fully. What a constructive attitude would reign in the boardrooms of industrial companies when they could plan with greater certainty. Their employees would feel more job security, and training programmes would become an essential investment rather than a discretionary expense to be jettisoned in bad times. And how much better the bankers would sleep at night, if they could add up real profits during the day and not suffer nightmares brought on by an endless stream of bad debts with every downturn.

Is this relative economic Utopia a mere pipedream? This book seeks to point a way towards such a reality. In the belief that the current welter of economic theories, data and jargon have obscured the fundamental issues, it is written deliberately in a simple style. It includes six telling graphs from the Financial Statement and Budget Report 1992-93 (the *Red Book*). Other statistics and data are kept to essential headline information taken mainly from the UK National Accounts (the *Blue Book*) and from information in the public domain. This is because the interpretation of current economic data is arguably based on false perceptions of the actual structure of the economy. This book therefore aims to present self-evident and commonly accepted facts to support the arguments for a reappraisal of the actual economic structure and the appropriate policies to manage it. The aim throughout has been to simplify rather than to elaborate, to reveal the essential points clearly rather than to enter into confusing detail, and to sketch out the outline of the wood rather than to get lost in the myriad trees planted by rival economists. Consequently, this book seeks to enumerate the fundamental principles of economics as the text proceeds. More ambitiously perhaps, it concludes with a blueprint for a programme of practical policies which are aimed to set the fundamental conditions to make the British economy work.

London   S.R.H.
16 October 1992

1

The Two Primary Factors of Production

The first principle of economics is that the man-made world is brought forth entirely from the earth. This applies to everything in creation, whether it is animal, vegetable or mineral. At the end of the natural span of life, everything returns once again to the earth, for as the churchmen say: 'Dust to dust....' The earth is not a muddy substance. On the contrary, it is animate, full of life and gives birth to every living organism: mankind, the other animal species, including the birds and sea creatures and the micro-organisms. Whether they are womb-born, egg-born, sweat-born or moisture-born, they are all the offspring of Mother Earth. The first natural law of economics is that everything in the man-made world comes from the earth and returns to her.

This is so obvious that you might think it hardly worth stating, let alone in a book about economics. The earth is, however, more than just the mid-wife of creation. She is more akin to a great spirit. She is in fact a heavenly body and the mother of all that has been, of all that is and of all that is to be. As a heavenly body she has her allotted station in the cosmos. She is never lacking in energy. She never ages or decays. She fulfils her role effortlessly, for with her no energy is ever expended. She requires no support, yet she supports all. This is formulated by the Law of Conservation of Energy, which states that energy in the living sphere of earth can neither be created nor destroyed.

This is not such an obvious statement as the first natural law, but surely, you say, it applies to physics rather than to economics. It does apply to economics in a very real way, however, because the implication is that everything mankind needs for its economic life is already and always existing and available. In fact, the intelligence of the earth goes far beyond energy as life-force, for she measures out the eternal procession of the four seasons, which provide for the sowing and harvesting of all crops, by rotation on her axis round the sun. She measures out the tidal movements of the oceans by her interaction with the moon. She forms the weather patterns by her interaction with the sun. So the third fundamental principle of economics is that the bounty which is given freely by the earth is for distribution to meet the community's needs.

Land is the first primary factor of production. The second is mankind's labour, in all its dignity and variety. These two combine as the universal

14

feminine and masculine forces respectively to form everything in the man-made world. The aeroplane in the sky, with its complex fuel, power and electronic systems and its crew and passengers, all come from the earth. Whereas the skill of the pilot consists in the safe delivery of passengers, the practical economist must have the skill to manage the balance between the two primary factors of production, land and labour, for the safe delivery of our economic requirements. The pilot must understand the principles behind the laws of flight and be able to interpret the cockpit instrumentation. The practical economist must understand the principles behind the laws of economics and be able to identify and interpret relevant data. The pilot must also navigate the aircraft along its flight-path to its destination. The economist must know where the natural economic cycle is leading in order to maintain the necessary balance in the two primary factors of production and then in the competing claims on the wealth that is produced by them.

Unlike the earth, whose nature is forever giving without fear or favour, people's natures and personalities are always changing. At one end of the spectrum we experience the lively and enquiring state of mind, which is open to understand the natural laws and relationships for the good of all. At the other end we experience the dull and unenquiring state of mind, which replaces interest in the natural laws with personal considerations of what is good only for the individual. Man can either work within nature's framework or fail to recognise that it even exists and so stumble around in the dark. These two archetypes, however, live in each of us, with greater or lesser strength from day to day. Each human life is an odyssey where the individual's nature is either refined or coarsened. It is the same with a nation's economy, for each generation has the chance to improve it or reduce it, to leave it solvent or bankrupt for the next generation. At the level of a nation, all this depends on whether the 'Creative Person' or the 'Degenerate Person' has the upper hand within society, for both tendencies inhabit each of us.

This is not a book about psychology, but it is important to acknowledge the erratic nature of man in contrast to the constant nature of the earth. The practical economist must allow for the former and understand the implications of the latter. The formulation of the gamut of human nature as an antithesis between Creative Person and Degenerate Person may not satisfy everyone, but the terminology itself does not really matter in the context of an enquiry into economics. The only thing that is important for this book is that you have some idea of what I mean by the phraseology. Everyone would agree that the late eminent scientist, Dr Albert Einstein, is at the opposite end of a scale to the late disgraced publisher, Robert Maxwell. The former gave us the Theory of Relativity and much else besides, while the latter perpetrated the single biggest theft in history by a single individual. By way of analogy, a public-spirited person formed the Saints and Sinners Club of London, as a clone of the New York club, in 1946. Those who are lucky enough to attend the annual dinner have to consult their own conscience and choose whether to wear a white rose or a red rose for the evening, thereby advertising whether they are a saint or a sinner. The point is that everyone is a saint sometimes and a sinner at some other times. The terms Creative Person and Degenerate Person are used merely to denote the gamut of possibilities inherent in human nature. They are not terms necessarily implying adulation or condemnation of individual characters, in terms of white and black, but rather they are economic terms differentiating the vision that encompasses the common good as opposed to blind self-interest.

In simple terms of economics the enquiring and open mind of the Creative Person seeks out the natural laws and how to apply them. This person is never greedy and gives regularly to charity; is always ready to help friends and colleagues and give what can be given; refines professional skills, craft or trade and delights in serving clients or customers. He or she never knowingly produces shoddy work or handles poor-quality merchandise, for the client's or customer's satisfaction is their satisfaction and source of energy, while money is merely a medium of exchange. Such people are happy in their work and life until the day they die.

The dull and blind intellect of the Degenerate Person is greedy and lustful and thinks mainly of the individual's own advantage. This person pollutes the environment without even thinking. Unthinking, he or she has no time to acknowledge that natural law even exists and still less time for those who do. They become governed by bad thoughts and engage in swindles, false accounting, ill-conceived hostile takeovers. They break securities' laws, plunder employees' pension funds and buy influence with their ill-gotten gains. They raise their own salary at a much faster rate than their employees and at the same time announce massive lay-offs. (The Chairmen of British Telecom and General Motors actually did this in the recession of 1991. The former, recognising the injustice, donated his entire salary increase to charity. The latter closed twenty-one factories involving 74,000 job cuts and at the same time drew his salary increase. He became widely discredited and the target of much national abuse. Hollywood even made a film about him, which was far from adulatory.) When the Degenerate Person dies, he does so unmourned by those whom he has misled or wronged.

Compared to the unchanging nature of the earth, which provides everything mankind needs without complaint or reward, human beings come in all shapes and sizes, and with many basic needs, appetites and desires. The more degenerate people get, the more they want. This seems to be the basic rule of Degenerate Persons. Creative Persons, on the contrary, eschew great riches in favour of a moderate amount of wealth, where they also tend the creative side of their nature: for example, in appreciation of the arts and other intelligent studies, not just with monetary donations, but in practice. Nevertheless everything that is brought into existence in the man-made world is produced by the application of labour on land. These two essentially different factors of production combine together as the first two primary factors of all production. The fourth fundamental principle* is that the man-made world and everything in it is entirely the result of labour on land, or labour applied to raw materials and substances extracted from beneath its surface. This principle is so obvious that it hardly seems worth spelling out. It appears so simple on paper, but the implications in the realm of economics are prevalent throughout every facet and every transaction of today's developed economies. What is not at all obvious, however, is identifying the effect of this law and its implications for macro-economic management, which is the real issue to be addressed.

* A schedule of Ten Fundamental Economic Principles is set out in Chapter 14.

Insert 1

Notice on a pure cotton designer shirt wrapper manufactured in Bangladesh

---

MAKE MOTHER EARTH HAPPY. BUY THIS SHIRT.

Did you know that in the time it took you to unwrap this shirt, 50 acres of tropical rain forest were destroyed. Americans threw away 41,666 plastic bottles, produced 242 tons of garbage and cut down 1,617 trees for paper. By choosing to buy this garment you have helped reverse this destruction and have contributed to the health of Planet Earth. We used no toxic chemicals, cleansers, bleaches or dyes to soften or colour this fabric. There is not a stitch of plastic in our product or our packaging. We only use recycled paper and our fabrics are all natural. Thank you for doing your part to protect our future. Your Mother thanks you too.

Footnote: This is an example of Creative Person manufacturing in a third world country, working within the natural structure for the benefit of the business, its employees, suppliers and distributors and making the customer happy. The cost in 1991 of this quality, pure cotton, designer shirt (from Bancrofts in New York) was only the equivalent of three cans of premium lager!

2

The Natural Economic Cycles

The earth and all her offspring are governed by natural life cycles. The rise and fall of each person or creature is in itself a cycle. Ancient cosmology even traces the cycle of the four ages – the golden, silver, bronze and iron ages – over millennia. These greater cycles are the proper study of cosmologists, astronomers and their analogues, but economists should note the presence of these greater cycles as a backcloth to the study of the natural cycles' interaction with the man-made world. The greater cycles are traditionally governed by the number 9 as multiplier. In the ancient astronomy and cosmology of India, for example, the number 9 represents the full and glorious manifestation of the earth. We do not need to rehearse the evidence here, but simply accept the rule of the number 9 as a guideline while we examine recent economic evidence. The number 9 will then either stand or fall on the empirical evidence.

The proposition is therefore that the number 9 in terms of solar years governs the basic economic cycle. This gives rise in a developed economy to the regular and natural pattern of expansion and contraction, of movement and rest. With the reconstruction and growth of the developed economies since 1945, this short 9-year cycle has become transparently obvious. The cycles of the economies of the Group of Seven (G7) – that is America, Britain, Canada, France, Germany, Italy and Japan – have increasingly converged in the post-WW2 era. This 9-year cycle, however (give or take a year for natural or man-induced distortions), is not oscillating between straight parallel lines. It is set against a 90-year cycle (give or take up to a decade for the distortionary effects), which itself rises and falls. Consequently, the sequence of short 9-year cycles is itself rising and peaking after about 45 years, being the mid-point or peak in the 90-year cycle, so that in the descending curve of this long cycle the short-cycle troughs go deeper and the upward recoveries are weaker. Finally the short and long cycles are set against the great 900-year cycles (give or take up to a century or more for major distortionary and cataclysmic events such as prolonged wars, plagues and famines), which govern the time-span of the rise and fall of nations and civilisations. Examples of the great cycles might include the birth of Greek philosophy in the sixth century BC, through the spread of Christianity and the work of the early

19

Christian fathers, culminating with Plotinus in the third century AD. Alternatively, the millennium from the time of Caesar's invasion of Britain in 55 BC to the Norman Conquest in 1066 may be cited. In this great cycle the distortionary variation of nearly 200 years could be taken as the period before and after the 100 years of internal warfare from 731 to 829, when England underwent a truly dark age in its history, when no one could expect to reap the crop that they had sown. For practical purposes of economics, however, the great cycles are not especially relevant, but a good working sense of the natural cycles most definitely is, particularly the interaction of the long cycle on the short cycle, which is so often overlooked by modern practitioners.

A Russian economist, Nikolai Kondratieff, who was born in 1882, first formulated the concept of a 'long wave' from his studies of the rise and fall of agricultural production. It was no doubt very difficult in his lifetime to detect any short-term rise and fall in the Russian economy generally. The difficulties of gathering meaningful data in that vast country most probably reduced the accuracy of the exercise. Nevertheless he proposed three periods as examples: namely, the 1780s to 1844-51, which peaked around 1817; 1844-51 to 1880-96, which peaked around 1870; and 1890-96 to 1914-20, when the Bolshevik revolution of 1917 was the cataclysmic distortionary factor which affected and is still affecting the Russian economy up to the present time. Thus he placed the troughs around 1745, 1790, 1844 and 1890, indicating another trough around 1930, the year of the Great Depression. Kondratieff's 'long waves' fell into 45-year spans, which is half the 90-year span that I have chosen to adopt. The two views are not necessarily incompatible. The fact that he failed to define the shorter 9-year cycle may cause doubts over whether his 45-year cycle was in fact only the first half of the full 90-year cycle, in that he assumed that the downturn at that the end of the first 45-years was the end of a 'long wave' and not the mid-point or peak before the actual long cycle of ninety years itself turned down. Those who draw a parallel between the 1991-92 recession as it develops into a slump and the Great Depression of the 1930s are not necessarily incorrect in assuming a 45-year cycle, but it is a 45-year cycle on the back of the upward curve only of a true 90-year long cycle. When the long cycle peaks, the short cycle recession at that point coincides with the downturn of the long cycle. The combined resultant force may thus appear as the end of a longer cycle of 45 years or so. The danger is that there may then be a failure to realize that the next 45-year long cycle is actually the second half of the 90-year long cycle, which is going to be on the back of the downward curve only of the true long cycle. This may not otherwise become apparent until the economy enters the

Graph 1: Business Cycles – World Trade in Manufactures and G7 Industrial Production 1970-93

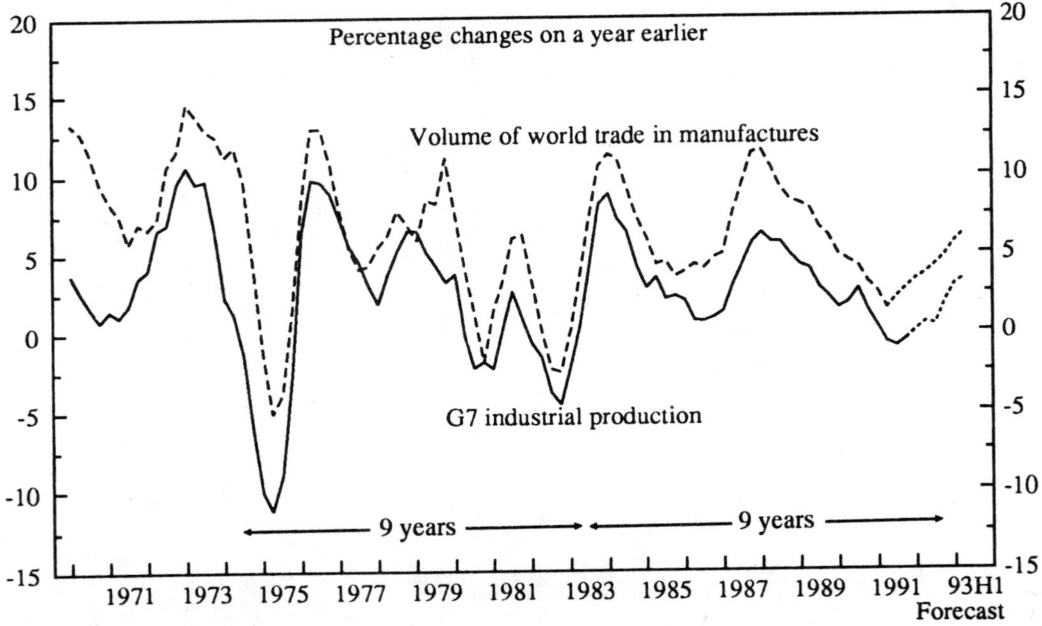

Percentage changes on a year earlier

Volume of world trade in manufactures

G7 industrial production

9 years

9 years

1971 1973 1975 1977 1979 1981 1983 1985 1987 1989 1991 93H1
Forecast

20 15 10 5 0 -5 -10 -15

Source: HM Treasury *Red Book*, 1992-3 (9-year cycles added).

third or fourth short cycle on the downward curve of that long cycle. By then it is too late to make the necessary changes in macro-economic management before the whole system well and truly hits the buffers.

A French physician, Clement Juglar, first formulated a short 8-year cycle in 1860, although his followers have argued for 9- and 10-year cycles. (This falls more neatly into the definition I have favoured of a 9-year short cycle, give or take a year for natural or man-induced distortions.) Subsequent analysis has tended to designate the crisis points in the short cycle as 1825, 1836, 1847, 1857, 1866, 1873, 1882, 1890, 1900, 1907, 1913, 1920 and 1929. At this point the longer cycle touched bottom as well and broke the step of the short cycle, first with the Great Depression and then with WW2. The important point is not whether the cycles are of 8 years, 10 years, 45 years or any other number of years, but rather to allow into the thinking and feeling processes the fact that there are short, long and great cycles. That awareness in itself makes us sensitive to where the economy stands in relation to the cycles (see Graph 1). At the present time, in 1992, it is particularly important to appreciate that the short cycle appears to have turned down at the same time as the long cycle.

Kondratieff was imprisoned for his attempts to show that nature rather than the Politburo governed the economic cycles. He died, it is not known when, in prison at the hands of totalitarian Soviet Degenerate Persons. Juglar's and Kondratieff's research, however, sparked a debate that the Creative Person has continued to this day. Schumpeter, for example, an Austrian economist who was a Professor at Harvard in the 1930s, claimed that the upswing was caused by new inventions and processes being put into production. The upswing moved into growth when the new markets thereby created attracted competition from other producers. This inevitably led to over-supply, causing bankruptcy and recession. This and similar explanations, however, confuse results with causes by overlooking the first principles, namely that the short, long and great economic cycles are as innate to the earth as the monthly cycle is to the human female. A fifth principle of economics or natural law may be formulated: the earth measures out and regulates economic life with short and long cycles, which are governed by the number 9 and by the sum of 9 raised to the power of 2 plus 9 respectively, as measured in solar years. Just as the clockwork accuracy of the tidal system is governed by planetary forces which may still be blown off course by storms, deluges and high winds, so the short and long cycles are affected by natural or man-induced distortions.

The application of this law, as with the other first principles, is exceedingly practical. For those engaged in economic management, be they economists, bankers, businessmen, public/civil servants or politicians, it is essential to have a clear appreciation of where the economy stands in relation to the short 9-year cycle, and where that cycle stands in relation to the longer 90-year cycle. The cycles cannot be stopped by mankind, but it is possible to work knowingly within them. For example, the banker who lends most or all of the finance required for a 3-year property development late in the cycle and after values have risen strongly may find the bank's loan turns sour in the approaching downturn as rentals decrease and the capital value of the project is exponentially reduced. The politician who eases credit and taxation as the economy booms, seeking 'a dash for growth', will find that it merely magnifies the existing upturn and the negative effects of the inevitable downturn. If they do this just as the 90-year cycle is itself turning down, the results are likely to be near-catastrophic. For the sixth fundamental economic principle is that those who abuse the earth's nature by failing to observe her ways have to pay the appropriate penalty, one way or another.

These examples seem obvious enough, but amazingly politicians and bankers in many developed economies, especially in the English-speaking countries, have repeatedly made these very errors, and on a grand scale too, in every short economic cycle since WW2. This was never more so than in the 1983-1992 cycle (examined in some depth in Chapter 9) which occurred just as the 90-year cycle which began in 1945 had peaked and really was turning down. The approach of the Creative Person would be to restrain the economic upswing and pay down debt, so as to be in a position to reflate gently and take on debt in the downswing. Creative Persons help everyone in this way, as G7 production represents the lion's share of volume of world trade (see Graph 1). Politicians talk about the need for OECD countries to help the Third World in a practical way, but the skilful management of their own economies would yield the best results for LDCs as well. The Third World supplies minerals and crops rather than manufactures, so these econo-mies rise and fall (as Graph 1 clearly indicates) with the fortunes of the G7 economies. Unfortunately politicians throughout the democratic G7 world have a perverse habit of doing the exact opposite, which means that they have to take on too much debt in both the upswing and the downswing. The trouble is that some politicians are looking at the 5-year electoral cycle and not at the 9-year natural cycle. These Degenerate Persons manage the economy in order to preserve their own jobs rather than the jobs of their fellow citizens. Then democracy suffers too, as the electorate have only two choices between two people doing the same thing: namely trying to get the top job. Hence the interest of Mr Ross Perot's entrance into the 1992 American election.

A theoretical impression of each short-term cycle within a long cycle can be painted to illustrate the general cyclical nature of economic development. There will generally be ten short cycles within a long cycle, spanning nearly a century. Five of the short cycles will normally co-exist with the upswing of the long cycle and five with the downturn. In actuality, of course, the number of cycles and the cycles themselves will be affected by the natural and man-induced distortionary effects. Nevertheless the impression may convey the different characteristics of each decade. It might be useful mentally to link the first five short cycles to the years 1930 or 1946-1991, which represented the upswing of the long cycle. It is also worth remembering that the boom years in the early 1980s had an intensity that may be mirrored for a short time in the recovery in the first decade of the long cycle's downturn, and so on. In theory it should only be at the end of each long cycle that the possibility of a real depression occurs, but that assumes that neither nature's catastrophes nor mankind's mismanagement of themselves produce an economic cataclysm. These are big assumptions.

The first short cycle is often characterised by a real depression or slump. Unemployment is so bad that starvation is sometimes recorded. Nothing stirs. Confidence is banished. Bankruptcy is widespread. Suicides result from financial failures. Ships are laid up. Mines are closed. Factories and shops are boarded up. The stock market sinks, and banks are illiquid. Wages collapse, and interest rates fall to almost zero as there are no creditworthy borrowers or viable projects. New inventions do not come to market as there is no capital to put them into production and no buyers for the finished products. It is a bleak condition.

The second short cycle reveals a slight upturn that seems to come from nowhere. Someone decides that they just have to replace their car or electric fire. Someone else just has to buy a new suit. Suddenly these 'someones' accumulate and create demand, and manufacturers are caught with their stocks down. Amazingly, the factory finds it has the beginnings of an order book and has to go to the bank manager to secure some working capital. The production manager informs the directors that if the profit earned on this stream of orders is invested in a new machine, efficiency and profits will rise. Inventors see their ideas begin to be turned into products. Unemployment begins to fall. The pent-up demand of consumers spills over into a desire for more of life's necessities and even a few luxuries. People feel better. The economy is on the move, but then it pauses for what seems like a short breather as interest rates rise slightly as loan demand rises.

The third short cycle quickly picks up where the second cycle left off. Consumer demand and investment continue to rise and unemployment continues to fall. The recovery in manufacturing improves confidence to build fixed assets and the construction industry begins to stir. The bank manager finds that loans are actually turning over nicely, and confidence really is returning. Then the economy pauses again as interest rates rise as a result of loan demand. Confidence does not evaporate as predictions are made that interest rates will fall again within months and everyone can see that the next upturn is not even a year away. (In 1974, of course, the third short cycle ended with a bang rather than a whimper, when the world economy suffered from the distortionary effects of an explosion in energy prices after the Yom Kippur war. In Britain a trade unionist called Arthur Scargill rashly chose this precise moment to lead the miners out on what he thought would be a timely and opportune strike for vastly higher wages, but it inevitably led to the long-term decline of the coal industry. At the same time interest rates and inflation soared, and western stock markets collapsed as if in a major downturn.)

In the fourth short cycle the economy is really humming. New products in all shapes and sizes appear on the market. The advertising industry comes of age. What seemed like a luxury a decade or two before now becomes a necessity. Construction of all types of buildings and infrastructure proceeds apace. The range of services and innovations quickens. The economy turns down to catch its breath, and the fifth short cycle builds on the advances of the fourth. Stock markets and economic activity hit all-time highs. Buildings go up everywhere, and a compulsive desire to speculate in stocks and shares replaces prudent investment. There is an inherent danger at this point, however, as people think the good times will simply go on and on, so the downturn when it comes is greeted with dismay. Even the humour in British television advertisements becomes muted! It is a more severe downturn than any of the others, as the long cycle has itself also peaked and turned down. The saturation of markets, surplus manufacturing capacity and over-supply of buildings are now revealed for all to see. Price deflation sets in, and the downturn goes on for longer than normal.

In the downward half of the long cycle the recovery of the economy in the first short cycle emerges as reinvestment and consumer demand slowly recover. For a short time it even seems that the economy has recovered to the glorious growth of the fifth short cycle, although unemployment persists at higher levels and the over-capacity problems are not fully resolved. The first recession on the long downturn soon removes such fond imaginings and the economy really struggles to pull itself out of the dive. It now becomes apparent that all the unsolved problems of the boom years – namely inflation, bad loans and over-capacity – conspire together to bring the economy down far lower than anyone can remember. Unemployment soars, and civil unrest and crime become widespread. The recovery takes an agonisingly longer time to reappear, and when it does so it is weak and anaemic and never reaches the level of activity recorded in the previous recovery. It becomes starkly apparent at this point that the economy is in a long-term decline, and this causes confidence to evaporate, so that the next cycle of the downswing goes even lower. The next recovery only turns out to be horizontal rather than rising. It hardly even manages to get out of bed! Then the economy takes its final dive into the last of the short cycles, which has the potential once again to end in a depression, with the threat of widespread bankruptcy and unemployment.

None of the gloomier aspects of depression, however, are entirely unavoidable. There is no inherent reason why the system should inevitably end up once again in widespread insolvency and unemployment. If it is realised that the way creation moves is in cycles, from rest to rest, there is no reason why Creative Persons cannot overrule the insatiable demand of Degenerate Persons for growth at all costs and in all seasons, and approach macro-economic management with a view to working knowingly within the cycles. The first step is to appreciate that this really is the way nature works and then to monitor and chart the economy's course. It really is not necessary for so many bankers and economists to fall into every elephant trap of recession that comes along, with the consequent damage to the economy that the rest of us, as tax-paying members of the public, have to pay for one way or another.

There is an important aspect of the business cycles to be noted, particularly in the remarkable ability of the capitalist system to invent and market new products, and that is the effect of technological advances, which often drive the recovery phase in the short-term cycles. In fact major advances in an economy are often linked to breakthroughs in transportation. It seems that the ability to move people and products either to more destinations or more quickly or more cheaply is the major growth factor. The age of steam opened up the vast continent of America, for example, so that the economy really did operate from coast to coast. This in turn opened up trade around the Pacific Rim in a way which the age of the horse could not even have imagined. Then the advent of the motor car and truck was perhaps the biggest single spur to worldwide economic growth ever seen. The jet engine was the next major innovation in transport, which linked countries and markets as never before.

Since WW2 economic growth has been quickened by a host of technical advances: for example, by the introduction of the ubiquitous computer. The early computers, during and after WW2, were powered by mechanical and electrical relays. Analogue coils were also used, and still are in applications capturing ultra sound inputs. Then, in the mid 1950s, transistors became the basic component. These in turn led to the introduction in the 1970s of digital converters. During the 1980s the speed and scope of digital hardware became so great that software development became the next great leap forward. The sheer power of the latest hardware has led to technological advances in semi-conductors, storage devices and advanced systems for rapid access to data, such as laser discs. The next generation of computers is already heading towards artificial intelligence. These great technological advances of Creative Persons generate whole new industries and sub-industries that provide the impetus for growth and jobs. They also require massive capital, which is more easily available in the upswing of the long cycle. In terms of macro-economic management it is essential that industry has equal access to capital in the downturn of the long cycle. If it doesn't, the downturn is accentuated, as recovery finds it harder to obtain the necessary impetus. If the capital is frittered away in the property markets, as it was in the 1970s and 1980s, it has the double negative effect of depriving industry of capital at exactly the time when the economy most needs the added impetus that only new technologies, processes and know-how can provide. The dearth of such capital and new technologies during the current worldwide recession of the early 1990s is evident. It is just as loud a warning bell as the massive loss of speculative capital and loan capital in the rapidly deflating property markets across the globe.

At the time of writing, in the summer of 1992, the Anglo-Saxon economies, namely America, Britain, Canada and Australasia, had been in actual recession in practically every sector for more than a year and were being joined in recession by Germany, France, Italy and Japan. In fact all the G7 economies were in recession of one kind or another in the second half of 1992, an ominous convergence that poses the threat that in the next cycle the G7 economies may rise and fall together, making a global depression all the more likely at the end of the next 9-year cycle. The previous recession in the Anglo-Saxon economies was in 1981-82, which in Britain severely hit the Midlands' manufacturing base. Before this, the Anglo-Saxon economies were in recession in 1974-75, after the first oil crisis of 1974, which in Britain triggered the collapse of the property market and the tertiary and secondary banks which had financed it with short-term money. Previously recession had struck in 1965 and in 1957-58, as the Anglo-Saxon economies recovered from WW2. These two post-WW2 recessions were not so apparent in Germany, which was financed directly by America through the Marshall Plan (and indirectly by Britain as it repaid war loans to America), or in Japan. Both these countries worked hard for reconstruction after WW2. These economies recovered strongly after the devastation led by their construction and engineering industries which required massive employment. The German construction industry helped lead the 'German economic miracle' in the 1960s, but it too collapsed in the 1974-75 recession, when the oil crisis hit an already slowing economy. The Japanese economy, which depends entirely on imported oil and gas, also contracted for three consecutive quarters in 1974, but did not fall in the 1980-81 downturn at all.

British manufacturers, for example, managed their export strategies in the 1960s to take advantage of other European economies which were still growing while Britain was in recession. The 1974-75 recession upset this reactive approach, however, as the Oil Crisis hit the worldwide economy, but the resultant boom in Middle Eastern and other oil-producing countries created enormous markets overnight, and the new price of oil also triggered exploration and production in the North Sea, Alaska and elsewhere. The recession in the early 1980s did not have a global implication, but the slump in the early 1990s most certainly did. It is highly significant that 45 years had elapsed since the end of WW2, which was the last cataclysmic distortion after the worldwide depression of the early 1930s. In fact, the short cycle between 1981-82 and 1991-92 coincided with the peak of an underlying long cycle causing the ensuing recession to be both deeper and more global than any post-WW2 recession. It also means that the recovery from this recession will take longer and appear more anaemic, and will be led by certain sectors rather than across the board, as the long cycle turns down and the short cycle struggles to turn up.

3

The Third Factor in Production and Distribution

Land and labour, as we have noted, are the first two primary factors of production. The third factor is the conditions in which the first two meet and under which production is distributed. For example, the world has recently witnessed the stark contrast in the capitalist and communist economic systems. Under these two very different sets of conditions, the same two primary factors of production have yielded completely different results, which have affected millions of lives, adversely and positively. The earth has obviously received the worst maltreatment under the communist conditions, and Soviet Degenerate Persons have their just reward: a poisoned environment. Not so obvious, however, is how capitalism has also made unwarranted assumptions about land. Capitalism's reward may well prove to be a global depression and collapse of industry, the banking system and government finances, if not in the recession which began in 1991, perhaps in a future recession. If the grotesque errors of the 1980s are (or could be) repeated on the same scale in the 1990s, that will almost certainly be the consequence in the next downturn. When an economy is on the bottom of a downturn, it is already too late for major correction, as the policy options are then severely restricted. The time to manage the downturn is in the preceding upswing, which is usually where the mismanagement occurs in the first place. By the time the downturn does arrive, however, most people have forgotten this. To demonstrate economic management in a practical way let us examine three simple models of completely different types of economy in the context of the interaction between the two primary factors of production, namely land and labour.

The simplest form of economic unity is a family or a collection of families, and for the purpose of this discussion let us call them by their first name, a tribe. The tribe is distinguished by its racial and cultural origins, by its language and customs. As an economic unit it naturally selects a chief who is responsible for the nourishment and protection of the tribe. He or she stands in relation to the tribe as the father or single parent stands in relation to the family. This simple structure can be found on every continent: the Red Indians of North America, the Amazonians of South America, the Scottish

29

clans, the African and Jewish tribes and in the various Chinese, Malay, Thai and Japanese tribes of the Far East. In fact the tribal unit still comprises a vast proportion of the world's population, even today.

There is another significant characteristic of a tribe, assuming it is not nomadic, which is that it holds unwritten sway over its tribal lands. Its homelands are sacrosanct to the tribe and it must of necessity fight to the death to preserve them. The tribe derives everything necessary for its existence from its land, and the good chief ensures fair distribution of all that is produced, on the basis of need or merit, or a combination of both. As the population of the tribe increases, the requirement for new territory naturally grows. If the land adjoining the homelands is freely available, the tribe simply expands on to it. The tribe will naturally select and appropriate the most fertile land next to its homelands. If, however, there is no free land adjoining the existing homelands, the possibility of a fight with a neighbouring tribe becomes almost inevitable. Hence the old tribal rule: 'Your neighbour is your enemy and your neighbour's neighbour is your friend.' It is starkly clear that the economic life of the tribe is inseparable from its occupation and cultivation of the land on which it lives. The two primary factors of production are inextricably linked.

There are other characteristics of a tribe which are relevant from the economic viewpoint. In its simplest form the tribe has no need of money as the chief receives all the produce and orders its distribution. No other medium of exchange is required. There is no need of credit either, as the allocation of tasks by the chief to short-term and long-term needs creates the tribe's own capital in the form of buildings, tools and improvements. Similarly there is no need for the payment of taxes, as the tribal unit must provide its own communal needs, such as defence. There is no rent payable as there is no landlord. Indeed there is no necessity for the legal ownership of land, as the whole tribe enjoys the fruits of its own homelands. And the most blessed relief of all is that there are no lawyers, as the chief is judge, jury and, if necessary, executioner! The tribe living on good cultivable land enjoys a happy and simple life, in tune with nature. Its biggest threats are invasion by famine or another hostile tribe. The encroachment of whites on to the Red Indian prairie homelands in the west of America is just such an example. It was in this exact situation that Chief Seattle gave his moving account of the Red Indians' deep understanding of the relationship between land and the tribe's ancestral enjoyment of that portion of the earth that was their traditional homelands. The sound of wisdom emanating from him as a Creative Person is as unmistakable as his description of the white pioneers as Degenerate Persons.

3. The Third Factor in Production and Distribution

Many readers will have read his stirring words elsewhere, so the passage quoted has been edited down to a few key sentences:

'One thing we know that the white man may one day discover: our God is the same God. You may think that you own Him as you wish to own our land, but you cannot. He is the God of man, and His compassion is equal for the redman and for the white. This earth is precious to Him, and to harm the earth is to heap contempt on its creator.

'When the last redman has vanished from the earth, and the memory is only the shadow of a cloud moving across the prairie, these shores and forests will still hold the spirits of my people, for they love the earth as the newborn loves its mother's heartbeat...

'We cannot buy or sell the sky, or the warmth of the land. We do not own the freshness of the air, or the sparkle of the water.

'Every part of the earth is sacred. Every shining pine needle. Every sandy shore. Every mist in the dark woods. Every clearing, every humming insect is holy in the memory and experience of my people.

'But to the white people one portion of land is the same as the next. The earth is an enemy which is there to be conquered. He kidnaps the earth for his children. He does not care. His appetite will devour the earth and leave behind only a desert... Whatever befalls the earth befalls the sons of the earth.'

These words of Chief Seattle, which embrace the six fundamental economic principles set out above, find an echo in the second economic system to be considered, namely the communist system. This may sound surprising, as in the West we tend to view the origins of the communist system as based on a fraud by the state at the expense of the citizen, both in terms of economic gain and in personal liberty. In fact the origins of the communist system, as exemplified by the former USSR, is much nearer the tribal system than is apparent at first glance. Before the Bolshevik Revolution in 1917 the Russian monarchy presided over a patriarchal system, where the father of the family acted in much the same way as the tribal chief. The family had its own portion of land, and all produce and income was handed to the eldest male member of the family, the patriarch. He distributed the total produce among the family in the same way as the tribal chief. As families migrated to the cities, those who stayed in the country sent food parcels to their urban relatives and received manufactured goods in return, a practice which continues today. Lenin's revolution simply determined to make the state the ultimate patriarch of the whole USSR, so that a centrally planned economy could be established in order to manage the change from a largely agrarian to a growing industrial economy. Under this new totalitarian system all land would be owned by the state, which would also receive all production and distribute it as the state determined. This system caught the imagination of the would-be revolutionaries, as it appeared manifestly fair and sensible. The state would simply become the patriarch. The problem was, was it workable? Lenin's Revolution overlooked two crucial factors. The first was mankind's inconstant nature, ranging from Creative Person to Degenerate Person and all shades in between. By replacing the family patriarch by the state a highly visible and local distribution system became continent-wide and therefore largely invisible and full of possibilities for Degenerate Persons to engage in corruption, favours, blackmarkets and threats, both on supply and distribution. Degenerate Persons were spurred on by the advantages to be gained by climbing the party hierarchy, as the party itself literally hijacked the greater part of the economic output. Consequently the state distribution system became corrupted, with an ensuing loss of any incentive even to work. The second major error in Lenin's thinking was that the five-year plans formulated by the state could in some way buck the natural economic cycles.

It was in fact Kondratieff himself who argued against Soviet Degenerate Person, in the form of Stalin, that this planned approach could not work as it failed to take the 'long waves', as he termed them, into account. The real problem for Kondratieff was that events soon proved him more right than the planned approach! As we all now know, Kondratieff was right and Lenin and Stalin were wrong. Unfortunately the western world now assumes that the inhabitants of the former USSR should, and will, now embrace a capitalist system. Whatever modifications are incorporated, the fact is that capitalism is fundamentally contrary to the deeply ingrained patriarchal system which is endemic to the Russian character. This is one example of why the economist needs to make allowance for the variable nature of mankind and of the specific nature of different nations for, as the old adage says, the leopard does not change its spots. (We talk of 'Mother Russia' and 'America, Land of the Free', and the two statements are saying something completely different about their respective peoples.) The probability is that the economy of the former USSR will work much better on the basis of local and regional co-operatives, segmented into appropriate industrial sectors. It is doubtful if the Russian character could accommodate a financial return to an unseen capitalist system, called a stock exchange. The current privatisation of vast tracts of industry, by giving ownership vouchers to the workers, will not fundamentally bring about a capitalist economy in the long run, because it fails to deal with the absence of real capital. Moreover the citizens of the former USSR have no middle class, so there is no trained population to run the complicated apparatus of a capitalist economy. In fact the necessary economic and other institutions and attitudes simply do not exist, as the demographic legacy of the communist party is only ranks of property-less state serfs. The distribution of ownership by vouchers will create fault lines across the patriarchal socio-economic foundations, as the vouchers will be worthless for the weaker economic units, but generate relatively wealthy citizens working in the successful sectors created by the former industrial-military command economy. The vouchers will cause envy and division, resulting in a loss of what little social cohesion there is. This could have dire consequences, which would be all the more tragic as the basic concept smacks of Creative Person at work, but the result may look like that of Degenerate Person before long. East European countries do have some economic institutions and a middle class and are in a better position to adjust, but the economic fate of the former USSR remains an ominous threat to Europe, the Middle East and China. The resources of the West will be better employed in advising on continent-wide distribution and exchange systems for crops, metals and manufactures, which can be made visible by electronic systems and therefore be seen to be fair and relatively free of corruption, rather than by trying to adjust this vast population to an all-out embrace of the market system.

The capitalist system has certainly out-performed the communist system in terms of supplying mankind's needs. The essential characteristic of capitalism is the free market, where every sort of produce and manufacture can be bought and sold at every stage of production. Each transaction normally represents a price at which the buyer is happy to buy and the seller is happy to sell. Each thinks they have secured a favourable deal. The profit motive provides the spur to the capitalist who has saved over and above his daily expenses to take risks and to reap the potential rewards. The system delivers a great variety of life's necessities and luxuries to consumers at a price which they are prepared to pay, such price yielding profit in the main to all those who worked to manufacture and distribute the finished article. The fundamental difference between the capitalist system and the communist or tribal systems is that within the capitalist marketplace the first two primary factors of production, land and labour, are treated like any other commodity. This simple assumption is an accepted fact, but it has enormous ramifications in the way the capitalist system works. For example, by parcelling out land as a marketable commodity capitalism reveals an asset with a value against which bankers will lend money. By treating labour as a commodity its market price at different levels of skill is determined by the law of supply and demand in the same way as fresh vegetables. By embracing the profit motive, the entrepreneur is created who requires a return on his investment. These conditions create the need for interest as a return to the saver and as a consequent cost to the borrower. The concept of capital and loans requiring dividends and interest inevitably arises in an economy which treats land and labour like any other marketable commodity. The ownership of land by one individual precludes any other individual from working on it, unless he pays an agreed rent.

These factors create the need for the capitalist entrepreneur to finance the evolving production, by investing from his savings. Savings are like any other commodity in a capitalist system, so they command their price too in the form of interest or other returns. The prophet Muhammad, for example, knowing that the nature of the Arabian as a desert nomad was essentially tribal, in his wisdom expressly forbad the charging of interest on any loans. The concepts of interest on savings and ownership of land, two essential characteristics of a modern capitalist system, let alone of a nomadic race, have no place in a tribal system. They have no place in the communist system either. This was made dramatically clear to some business colleagues on a recent trip to Russia to visit the giant aerospace works at Ul'yanovsk on the river Volga, 800 kilometres east of Moscow. The factory complex is spread over 40 square miles and includes a town with a population of 250,000. In fact the whole operation is a tribe of aerospace workers, with its chief executive giving the orders. The visitors were overawed by what they saw and stunned by what they heard. The Russians were not using modern aluminum-stretch technology, so one visitor asked what an actual wing cost. This question only produced blank looks. The visitors wanted to buy the whole of an Antonov 126 transporter, which has a lift capacity three times greater than anything in the West and the wing seemed an inoffensive place to start the ball rolling. The Russians, however, could not name a price. They could not do this as they did not know what anything had cost. The largest airplane in the world and it had no costings! The factory, they were told, paid no rent as there was no landlord. It had no borrowings as it had no obligations, so there was no interest. (Russian industry may not be efficient in the main, but at least it has no borrowings.) Wages were paid partly in state cash, but also in subsidies and vouchers, at the level determined by the state's job grades and pay scales. Materials and sub-systems were received from other state factories under the military command economy, just as if the tribal chief had ordered the tribespeople to defend the homelands. Unbelievably, whatever price was eventually sought, it would be a fixed price, as there was, officially at any rate, no inflation. And at the Farnborough Airshow in 1992 the Russians proved themselves contenders as the world's leading aerospace manufacturers with their MIG 29 fighters, Tupolev 204 civil airliners and advanced helicopters. They stole the show, while the Anglo-American manufacturers were left gawping. The privatisation vouchers being issued in Ul'yanovsk have acquired a real value, just as the shares in British Aerospace are losing value fast, partly as a result of an ill-judged attempt to join the property speculation band-wagon in the late 1980s. The absence of ownership of land in the communist system meant that the aerospace tribe at Ul'yanovsk got on with building world-beating aeroplanes. Degenerate Persons running British Aerospace overshadowed the Creative Persons designing and manufacturing its Harriers and Tornados and turned the group into big-time property speculators, and losers, as part of their so-called industrial strategy. Two different systems have produced, against the apparent odds, two completely different results.

The capitalist treatment of land as a marketable commodity which can be bought and sold and offered as security for a loan even by an aircraft manufacturer, creates various anomalies. Unlike finance provided by a bank to build a capital asset, such as an aircraft, ship or building, there is no increase in the sum total of production when a bank lends money purely against undeveloped land value. The purchaser of the land, who borrowed some of the money from a bank, pays over that money lent by the bank, together with his or her own money also to be invested in the land, to the vendor of that land. Then the vendor has the money for his or her land and has a monetary claim on the system's production. This claim will exceed the value of actual production by the amount of the consideration that was paid to the vendor by the purchaser for the land, as financed by the bank loan. This is nothing other than one of the many causes of the inflationary characteristic of the capitalist system, assuming always that the vendor did not reinvest that portion represented by the bank loan in another investment in land, or more precisely in something other than current production, and so on ad infinitum. Or, to put the matter another way, land purchases financed by credit create a purchasing

3. The Third Factor in Production and Distribution

power in the economy which is not backed by production and is therefore inflationary. True, the amount of inflation unleashed by the aggregate of such transactions may only account for a small proportion of the total of inflation at any one time. The purpose of the example, however, is to show how the workings of the land market are fundamentally different from markets dealing with produce and manufactures and the exchange of financial instruments, as British Aerospace is now discovering. In non-property markets it is very easy to see or find out who or which organisation(s) were the actual producers of value. But who creates the value in undeveloped land?

In the tribal and communist systems this question did not arise, for the simple reason that the land was held or deemed to be held in trust, as it were, for the whole population. There was no private ownership of land, and so there was no market in land. The fundamentally distinctive feature of the capitalist system is that it has always operated in a regime of total land ownership, where no further land is freely available, in which land has a price and can be bought and sold. As Chief Seattle observed: 'To the white people, one portion of land is the same as the next.' This is true of the context in which he meant it, but the capitalist also views each piece of land differently in the context of price, as each piece of land has a different value in the eyes of the market. This leads to the positive feature of the capitalist market in land, in that every piece of land can be scrutinised with a view to its optimum development for the benefit of the economy as a whole. You only have to compare a capitalist city with a communist city to see the relative effectiveness of the capitalist land market.

We are still left with our nagging question. Who creates the value inherent in the capitalist system in undeveloped land? Or rather, who creates the value of land itself, whether it is or is not developed? When a valuer places a valuation on a building the value could be expressed as being divided between the undeveloped land or the value of the actual site itself and the value of the actual building itself. The site value is simply the market value of the bare land. By deducting this site value from the total valuation, the actual valuation of the building on its own is determined. It is clear who created the value attaching to the building. It could only have been the developer, who worked with architects and other advisers to design it and also paid the builder to construct it. Sometimes the developer's profit is enhanced by obtaining planning permission on land purchased before it had attracted any such permissions. Sometimes it is enhanced by an additional 'marriage value', where the developer either acquired several adjoining sites and lumped them together or acquired a tenancy of a site and then purchased the freehold of the same site, at a discount to its market value as a consequence of the tenancy. Leaving aside the grey area of planning permissions and marriage values for the moment, it is none the less clear that the developer and no one else created the value of the building. But did the developer also create the site value in the first place? The answer must be 'no', because no individual or organisation ever created any site value. How could they?

The difference between site value and total value, between the value of the bare site and the value of the developed site complete with building, is made starkly clear by an unusual example. The deputy treasurer to King George V, Sir Ralph Harwood, made a hobby of buying and restoring Tudor houses. He bought a sixteenth-century manor, Walden House, in Saffron Walden, Essex. In 1935 he moved it – yes, moved it! – to West Grinstead in Sussex. Clearly both sites had residential planning permission and were therefore valuable. Each site had its own site value. These site values did not change, whether the house was on it or not. The site value at Saffron Walden did not go down when the house was taken down, and the site value at West Grinstead did not go up when the house was put back up. The site values did not change either when the house was on neither site during transportation. The house disappeared and reappeared, but the site value of each site did not. It couldn't, as it was inalienable from the land itself. What the astute royal treasurer had spotted was that the site value in Sussex was higher than the site value in Essex, so he moved the house.

The same phenomenon is observable in any other capitalist economy. If you were one of the small proportion of the world's population who travelled the twenty miles or so from Minneapolis airport to Wayzata and Lake Minnetonka to the west during the 1980s, you must have been struck by several factors. In 1980 you had to head north, skirt downtown Minneapolis and then head west on a busy road. The journey could take up to an hour or more. By 1990, however, a new road led directly west from the airport, and Wayzata was then less than half-an-hour away. The amazing feature of this new road was the increasing number of office blocks and business parks that sprang up overnight. Similarly if you drove downtown from Wayzata, the old road was rebuilt as an expressway and this journey time was also cut by more than half. Wayzata and the surrounding lake areas became more accessible. The whole area became more desirable as a result of the improved accessibility, in fact more like Sussex than Essex. House prices and building plots rose steadily in value. The former farmlands that found themselves alongside the new road from the airport became offices and factories and also rose in value. The airport traffic steadily increases and values seem set to go on rising as the economy grows.

There is nothing unique about Minneapolis, except perhaps the weather, which divides the year into two seasons, into road-building and winter, between adding site value to the land by expansion of the communal infrastructure and keeping warm! The same phenomenon of civic expansion can be witnessed anywhere else in the capitalist economies. In the 1970s, for example, the railway lines from London into the County of Kent were electrified and became more efficient. House prices along the line rose strongly as a consequence. In Kent at this moment, in 1992, despite the severity of the recession, there is still an active market in commercial properties around the small town of Ashford. Why? The largest civil engineering project in the world, the Eurotunnel, will have its terminal just outside the town, which will become a focal point for the two-way trade between the United Kingdom and Continental Europe.

Site values clearly rise as a result of the expansion of the economy as a whole. It is inevitable that when a new road, railway line or other useful facility is constructed, whether it is financed by public or private funds, the consequent improvement is reflected in higher values for adjacent sites. It is impossible that this could not be so. If you are in doubt, go and build a road or a bridge and watch the land around your improvement rise in value, but don't forget to buy this adjoining land before you announce your intentions! It sounds silly, but the world's largest real-estate developer recently made this mistake, as it were, the other way around. Olympia & York, based in Toronto, built the largest and best office block in Europe in a derelict dockland in East London, called Canary Wharf. In the 1992 property recession, the project went bust. The problem was not that Olympia & York invested around £1 billion in the development, but that nobody could get to it as there was no adequate access, either by road or by rail. They had agreed to provide £400 million as their share of the cost of building a new underground railway line from the centre of London to the docklands, the Jubilee Line, which was estimated to cost £1.6 billion in total and to be completed in 1995. When this new line is built you will be able to see the value of the Canary Wharf site, whether built on or not, start to rise in value even as the digging for the underground railway line begins.

Furthermore the site values around Canary Wharf and every planned station along the route will also start to rise for the same reason. The improved access translates immediately into higher site values and automatically accrues to the benefit of the site owners. The trouble with Canary Wharf is that it is some six miles from the centre of the City of London and its initial site value was most probably nil, at least without proper access. The construction of the new underground will clearly create site value, which will rise to match or exceed the developer's contribution to the cost of the whole railway line. The developer would hardly part with £400 million unless the assessments of the enhanced site value justified this level of outlay in the first place. The point is, therefore, demonstrated conclusively by this example that the community's expansion and improvements are directly reflected in enhanced site values, which may be accurately termed its 'community value'. Unlike the developer of Canary Wharf, however, the owners of most sites make little or no contribution to the cost of investment in the community's expansion and improvements. Who can blame them, if they can simply enjoy the enhanced site value and effectively receive the community value without paying for it?

The treatment of land as a marketable commodity in the capitalist system also creates an interesting opportunity for governments to levy taxation on the value created, whether by the community's expansion or by developers' expertise. Industry works on raw materials from the earth and adds value to them in the form of a finished product. Industry is taxed on its employees, fuels, premises and, profits and, indirectly, when its manufactures finally reach the end of the product chain and are purchased by consumers who pay Sales Tax in America and Value Added Tax in Europe. No one has ever made out a case that industry is under-taxed! Service industries from laundries and hotels to airlines are taxed in exactly the same way as regards the value they add for their consumers. Property developers pay indirectly for the taxes suffered by their professional advisers, and builders when they pay these costs to develop a site. They too are taxed on their profit when they realise their added value in the sale of the finished factory, warehouse, shopping precinct, office block or house. All these types of construction are necessarily built on land. Occasionally a daring property developer even acquires 'air rights' over an existing structure or railway station, but the building still has to have a footprint on the land.

What taxes does the developer or property owner pay on the added value in the land itself? This is what has been termed the community value, being the value of the site before it is developed, which is caused by the community's expansion and improvements. The developer only pays the same profits taxes as are paid by the manufacturing company, currently 35% in Britain. The developer keeps the other 65%, just like the manufacturer who really did add value. This distortion applies even more to individuals. In

3. The Third Factor in Production and Distribution

Britain, for example, nobody pays any tax on the profit from a sale of their principal residence. You can buy a house for £25,000 and sell it fifteen years later for £250,000 and you are not liable for any tax. When house prices are rising strongly in the upswing, this allowance creates a most unusual anomaly. I can well remember in the boom of 1972-74 lying in bed at night and conscious of the fact that I was earning more, tax-free, on the daily increase in the value of the house in West London I was sleeping in than I was earning, after tax, working in the daytime as a qualified professional in the City. This extraordinary phenomenon, of earning more asleep at night than by working in the daytime, of being turned into a Degenerate Person by rising house prices, posed many questions. Did it really matter? Or was this grotesque imbalance trying to tell everyone that there was a structural fault in this particular capitalist system? Nature does not like a vacuum and does not really approve of imbalances either. There clearly is something not quite right, in which case the imbalance must reappear at some point and exhibit a contrary effect.

In the downturns of 1974-75 and 1991-92, the exact opposite did in fact actually happen to property values. In August 1992, for example, the Bank of England issued a report claiming that over a million households in Britain were caught in a 'mortgage trap' and the number was rising daily. People's salaries and wages, after deduction of tax and after living expenses including mortgage interest and repayments, could not now provide savings at a fast enough rate to compensate for the drop in the value of their houses, which had now gone below the amount outstanding on their mortgages. If they sold their houses into the declining market to repay debt they were still left with a residue of debt that prevented them from taking up a new mortgage for their next house. They appeared to be well and truly stuck. Before they could move, whether to rent or to trade down, they were advised that they had to save the difference between the outstanding mortgage, often increasing with interest arrears, and the reduced value of their house, which was itself still declining as the market continued to drop, by 3.1% in just September 1992 alone.

Does this phenomenon of the mortgage trap matter or not? To the individuals involved it most definitely does matter. It also has a highly damaging effect on the rest of the industrial economy because consumers caught in the mortgage trap are forced to save by cutting their expenditures, thereby strengthening and lengthening the recession for industry as well. In July 1992, when John Major changed his advice and urged consumers to 'spend, spend, spend and not save', the nation saved instead a net £135 million in that month alone. It had no option. Its spending power had been blown on over-blown

40

property prices in the previous boom, financed by excessive credit and loan levels. Whereas in the 1980-81 recession consumer spending fell by less than 2% of GDP, in the current recession it has fallen 3.5% since mid-1990. Nor was this the extent of the problem, as the commercial property market was in a worse state than the residential market. The 1991 Annual Report of the Bank for International Settlements, adjusted for inflation and taking 1982 as a base, showed British residential property at end-1991 at 144, but commercial property at only 61. True, not so many individuals are directly affected by the state of the market for factories, shops and offices, but the effect of the downturn of the commercial property markets does affect them indirectly as it drags the whole economy down. For example, it will reduce the value of their pension plans which are invested in commercial property. The banks which financed the commercial developments lost heavily and then suffered severe liquidity constraints, thereby forcing property prices even lower, as would-be purchasers could not arrange financing even at the newly depressed prices.

Since the two primary factors of production are land and labour in the above descriptions of the capitalist system, which treats property as another commodity to be bought and sold like any other product, service or manufacture, it was abundantly clear that the condition of the property market seriously impinged on industry and therefore on the labour market. If the interaction at the third point, being the conditions in which labour is applied to land, are such as to create a structural imbalance between property and industry, the economy cannot work efficiently. If, in addition, the natural economic cycles are overlooked by the politicians, economists and bankers at the same time, the possibility of a major financial accident or melt-down, leading to depression, becomes a real possibility. The seventh fundamental principle of economics may now be formulated: the economic conditions under which labour is applied to land, being the third point, will determine the overall efficiency of the economy. The fact as stated is simple and even obvious, but a great deal more analysis of the interaction of property and industry under the actual conditions at the third point is clearly necessary.

4

Property vs. Industry in the Market Economy

In every economic system land and labour, as we have noted, are the two primary factors of production. This is simply a pragmatic fact of creation and is unalterable. In a capitalist system, as opposed to every other economic system, property and labour are treated as commodities like any other, which can be freely bought or sold in the marketplace. There is a fundamental distinction between these two primary factors of production, as has been discussed, in that the nature of any parcel of land is constant in its potentiality to provide what mankind needs, whereas individual nations, men and women are of varying natures, which are themselves often showing different facets of their character at different times. Land is finite and attracts to itself a value as the result of the community's expansion and improvements. Mankind's population is never static and has no economic capital value as such, as mankind can only extract its reward in a capitalist system from the market price for its labour, which is subject to the rule of supply and demand. The title of this chapter implies an inherent conflict between property and industry. In fact in a developed market economy every factor in production, whether it be property, labour, financial investments, public works, deposits, loans and even government borrowing are competing for the same available resources. It is this competitive characteristic of capitalism which is its most productive attribute, namely the incentive to be economically effective against competing forces. Capitalism does not brook idleness, incompetence or misallocation of resources. The same could not be said of communism, for example, which allows for idleness and inefficiency while at the same time engendering corruption and political servitude.

It has been shown that in a capitalist market economy the value of unimproved land and the site value of developed property increase by virtue of the expansion of a community and by communal improvements. This value has been termed 'community value'. Labour, or industry, adds value to the raw materials extracted from the earth by virtue of sweat and skill effectively organised to meet market requirements at a price the market will pay. It seems incongruent that property and industry should somehow find themselves in conflict with one another. In the natural structure of the economic universe it would seem that they would be designed to work in co-operation rather than in conflict, for it is by their combination that the man-made world comes into existence. In our model of the tribal system there was no inherent conflict between the tribe and its requirements and the land on which it lived. In this system, the two live together in the harmony spoken of by Chief Seattle. The complicated structure of the modern capitalist system has clearly imported elements which have subtly changed the relationship between land and labour as compared with the simple tribal system.

In the tribal system the tribe works together on land 'belonging' to the tribe as a whole to produce its requirements. In the capitalist system, however, land is 'privatised' and labour is hired and fired. Both land and labour are bought and sold in the capitalist marketplace like any other commodity. Just as in the structure of the living cell the DNA is shown diagrammatically as an intertwining double spiral, so in the structure of the capitalist economy property and industry interact in a never-ending succession. It may be argued, for example, that as industry satisfies the community's needs and drives economic expansion, so it adds value to the property in which the community lives and works. As property increases in value, so do the financial assets of that capitalist community from which further industrial growth can be achieved. There is nothing unnatural in this mutual relationship, as the one is directly consequent upon the other. There would be no industry without the raw materials from beneath the earth, and no increase in property value without the expansion of the man-made world across the earth's service. Property and industry do support each other and are not in any conflict. As properties increase in value, so the economic rent increases which industry has to pay. So what? Property values have risen as a result of the community's expansion and improvements, such as transport links, and this has benefited the particular factory in various ways. There is a growing and mobile workforce, and access to markets, both domestic and overseas, is enhanced. The growth in the industrial infrastructure brings new suppliers and services which enhance the area for various types of industry and further increase property values. The landlord of the factory, whether it is the capitalist entrepreneur in his or her own name, a property investment company, a financial institution or government agency, or even the factory's own pension fund, cannot ask for a rent that is higher than the market value; otherwise the owners of the business will move to premises that are offered at a current market rental.

4. Property vs. Industry in the Market Economy

The possibility of moving to a new site is fine in theory, but in practice there may well be restraints and complications. For example, the manufacturing company may have entered into a long-term lease, which ties it to the particular property for many years into the future; the factory building may be designed to the specific needs of a particular production process; the plant and equipment may well not be capable of operating efficiently after a removal; and finally there may be no suitable premises or land available at an economic rental. So, in practical terms, there may be many problems and additional costs in moving to alternative premises. On balance the landlord is usually in a stronger position than the tenant, particularly if the tenant has entered into a long-term lease. In Britain most commercial property is let out to tenants on twenty-five year leases. These leases are usually called 'full repairing and insuring institutional leases', meaning that the tenant pays the rent, repairs and insurance. They usually contain provisions for the rent to be reviewed by the institutional owner, upwards only, every five years. For properties located in prime positions, such as a warehouse near Heathrow Airport or office premises in the heart of the City, the rent is often reviewed, upwards only, every three years. These 'upwards only' rent reviews became pretty much a standard feature of commercial leases from the late 1960s and early 1970s, when inflation really set in. These standard provisions also operate in America for similar periods for the same reasons. In the much larger American economy, however, the national chains have been able to use their financial and market clout to take on the landlords and to avoid many of the punitive effects of long leases. Long before the property slump of the early 1990s American tenants had negotiated break clauses in their leases, say every five or even three years, whereby they could extricate themselves from the lease commitment; rental increases were often linked to a percentage increase of actual sales; and leases even contained options for the tenant to buy out the freeholder, sometimes on advantageous terms. Many British tenants are interested in bringing these characteristics of American leases into the British property market, but the large property companies and institutions are offering determined resistance.

Whereas the property owner is relatively well protected from inflation, the manufacturer suffers acutely. The factory has to replace raw materials and equipment at inflationary prices from historic earnings accumulated at lower price levels. The introduction of inflation into the capitalist system during and after WW2, however, did not have the same deleterious effect on the finances of landlords because the value of their property investments simply rose with inflation, as the usual terms of their 'institutional leases' meant that

44

they could recoup inflation through higher rents as each rent review fell due every third or fifth year. This process raised the capital value of their assets at least in line with inflation. Land and property of all types was a perfect hedge against inflation, whereas industry struggled to preserve its capital, which was ravaged by inflation, reaching double figures in the upward curve of the long cycle (see Graph 5 in Chapter 6). Quite simply, every time industry delivered a product that it had priced months previously when booking the order priced at X, it then had to replace the raw materials and components at X plus inflation. The same effect has also been inflicted on agriculture, where smaller farms, under 1,000 acres, have not been able to earn enough to replace ever more costly equipment, so farms have tended to increase in size as smallholders were squeezed out. Moreover, as salaries and wages lost their purchasing power on account of inflation, so the trade union monopolies exerted their power to seek higher compensation, not based necessarily on higher productivity but merely to regain parity before the ravages of inflation. As the nominal amount of salaries and wages increased for labour, so did individuals' capacity to borrow also rise in nominal terms. This fed through to the residential property market which rose rapidly from the mid-1960s in the developed economies. Quite simply, if a worker could borrow on mortgage two-and-a-half times his or her annual pay and their annual pay doubled over five years, the value of housing in nominal terms would rise in proportion, because the residential property markets are financed largely by personal long-term borrowings by way of mortgages. As inflation persisted after WW2, particularly in the 1970s and 1980s, the true repayment cost of existing mortgages was in fact reduced by the continuing inflation, which still drove salaries and wages to higher levels, which in turn fed into yet higher prices for residences and for undeveloped land suitable for building. In these intertwining spirals of wage pull / cost push inflation, of wage-rise / property-rise / mortgage-rise / cost-rise inflation, the manufacturer suffered and the landlord prospered. The cause of inflation will be reviewed in Chapter 6, but it is already clear that one of its effects is to raise property values, rental costs and the reward to labour in nominal terms, in a potentially never-ending spiral at the expense of manufacturing's historic capital base. As the latter declines, so does investment and employment, driven out by the forces operating in the property markets, sending values ever higher.

It is easy to see how the inflationary spiral described above causes inflation in property values. The presence of sophisticated property markets means that this value can be realised, if not with the speed of shares on a stock market, at least with a degree of reliability. Consequently the banking community has come to view property assets as a prime form of security for short- and long-term loans, as property values have risen since WW2 with only the occasional hiccup, as in 1974-75, when the stock market also collapsed, and in 1991-92. Bankers decided to lend higher and higher percentages of the market value of property. They made little distinction between the site value of bare land and an actual development. They were both suitable for property loans and in most years their value rose strongly, through inflation, through the 'upwards only' rent review clauses of commercial properties and through higher salaries and wages driving the residential market. The increasing loans from the banking community secured on property themselves drove property prices even higher, as the availability of easy credit on a massive scale fuelled the various property markets. These developments affected industry adversely in a number of ways. First, the rise in property prices forced rents to go even higher, although yields may have been falling, particularly in the upswings of the short cycles. Secondly, manufacturing industry had to compete with property markets for valuable working capital from the banks. Thirdly, labour had to compete against itself to secure employment in a dwindling market, dragged down by a declining manufacturing sector.

Table 1: Britain's GDP and the Decline of Manufacturing
£0,000,000,000 (billions)

	1970	1980	1990
Agriculture, forestry & fishing	1.3	4.2	7.1
Energy & water supply	2.1	19.4	24.3
Housing rents	2.4	12.1	30.7
Other services	4.5*	10.7	31.0
Government services, including defence	2.9	14.5	31.5
Transport & communication	3.7	14.6	34.0
Construction	3.1	12.3	36.0
Education & health	2.3	18.0	45.1
Distribution, hotels & catering; repairs	4.8	26.0	70.2
Banking, finance, insurance (net)	1.5	14.7	60.6
Sub Total	28.6	146.5	370.5
Manufacturing	**14.9**	**53.6**	**107.0**
All industries	43.5	200.1	477.5
Manufacturing as %age of all industries	**34.3**	**26.8**	**22.4**
%age rate of decline, per decade	–21.9–	–16.4–	?

* Less stock appreciation of £1.1 Bn.
Source: *U.K. National Accounts*, 1991 Edition, 2.1 and 1979 Edition, 3.1

4. Property vs. Industry in the Market Economy

The fact that industry was losing out in the race with property is borne out by the post-WW2 experience of the American and British economies in particular. The Japanese economy actually demonstrated the opposite in the 1980s, with booming property markets and booming industry, with capital investment per employee at three times the level of Britain. The day of real reckoning for property prices in Japan has not yet dawned and may even be postponed until the next recession, although the first reductions in values since the National Land Agency started in 1975 have been recorded at under 5%, but with larger falls of 12% in Tokyo and 23% in Osaka. Immediately after WW2 the American and British economies were largely industrialised and their manufacturers commanded world markets for their products. Manufacturing industry in Britain has declined so far that it is now reckoned to be only 22.4% of GDP (see Table 1). This is a desperate and dangerously low percentage for a developed economy, let alone for one supporting a population of over 57 million people on a small island (see Graph 2). It has been in continuous decline since 1971, and employment has fallen since 1979 by 36%, from 7.1 million jobs to under 4.5 million in 1992. Britain now suffers a deficit on trade in manufactured goods for the first time since the Industrial Revolution. Until WW2, Britain cruised along on the back of its industrial pre-eminence and the empire was its customer and there was no real competition. Since WW2, however, the world has changed. The empire has gone, and fierce foreign competition has replaced it. Now the fiscal distortion at home is threatening to sink what's left of the manufacturing base. When North Sea oil runs out early in the next century Britain's plight will be desperate, unless the economy is refocused on industry rather than on services and property. Nor is the position in the long term any better for the giant American economy, on which Britain depends so much, for there manufacturing industry accounts for approximately 30% of GDP. The American economy is only less than a decade or so behind the British economy in the long-term decline of its manufacturing base. Both economies have suffered in much the same way in recent years and for very similar reasons. There is only one viable future for the American and British economies, and for most developing economies, and that is industrial recovery through rediscovery of the natural balance between land and labour. Higher land values in themselves are of absolutely no use in this battle. They are only of short-term use to the hard-pressed bankers and their over-borrowed customers (see Graph 3).

Graph 2: Britain's Industrial Problem – UK Volume Share of World Trade in Manufactures 1970-93

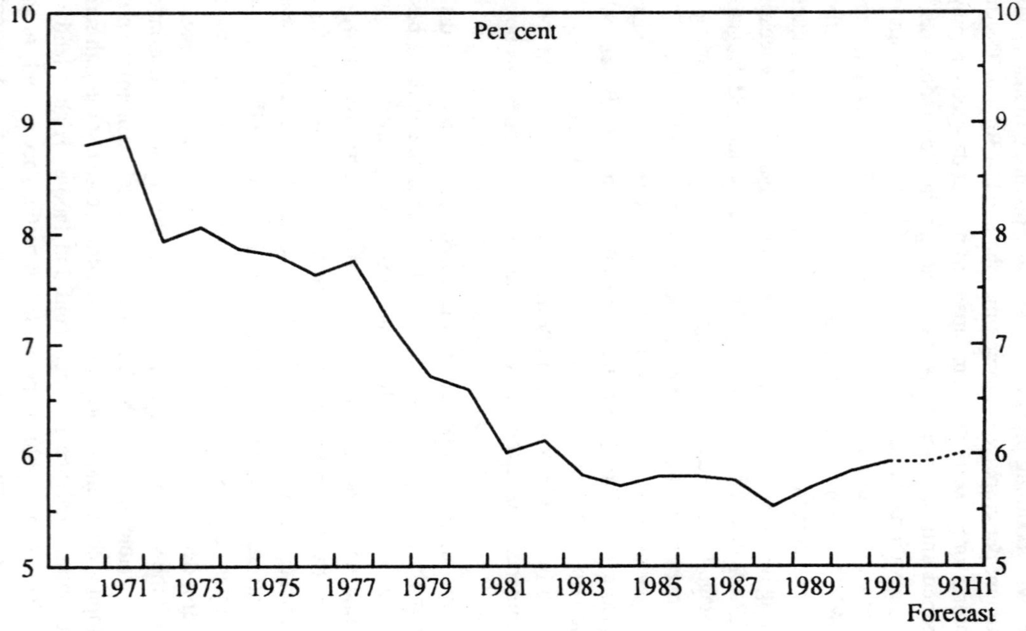

Source: HM Treasury *Red Book*, 1992-3.

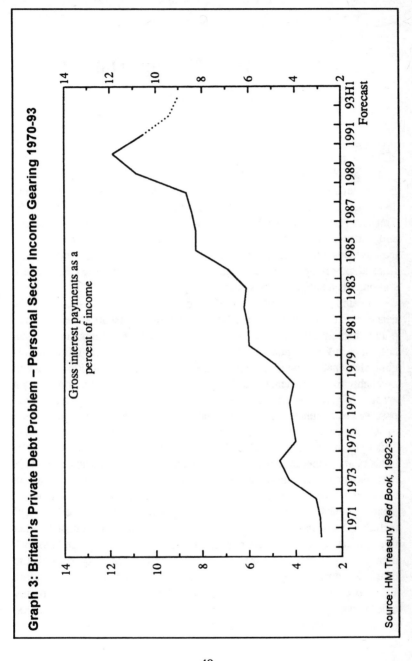

Graph 3: Britain's Private Debt Problem – Personal Sector Income Gearing 1970-93

Gross interest payments as a percent of income

Source: HM Treasury *Red Book*, 1992-3.

49

5

The Problems of Corrupt Data and Corrupt Attitudes

Investigations of the monetary measurements of the conditions at the third point are generally hampered by the lack of complete and accurate data and by the presence of corrupt data. For example, when the Chancellor of the Exchequer announced in his autumn statement in the House of Commons in 1991 that 'recovery was just around the corner' most people other than the Treasury Mandarins knew he was wrong. The taxis, hotels, pubs, restaurants and shops in London were visibly deserted, and most businesses were experiencing a tangible reduction in order books and levels of employment, from stockbroking to airlines through to the factory floor. The UK Treasury computer had simply got it wrong – yet again!

To demonstrate the problems posed by corrupt data, let us examine the data behind the single most important factor influencing worldwide economic policy, namely inflation. During the 1980s the doctrine of monetarism took hold in both Washington and Westminster as the way to curb inflation. It is quite clear that if money is simply printed and put into circulation prices will inevitably rise as an increasing amount of money seeks to purchase a constant amount of goods. In simple terms, monetarism was the concept that, if you observed and counted the amount of money in circulation, you would be able to see and calculate what was going to happen to inflation down the road. This in itself would be useful, as inflation erodes the historic capital base of industry and is therefore itself clearly one of the causes of the other twin evil, unemployment. The problem for the monetarist is how to keep a constant watch and how to count the money. M0 is defined as 'narrow money', meaning notes and coins in circulation, whereas M4 is 'broad money' including bank and building society deposits and loans and a host of other financial instruments. In very simple terms M0 is 'walking around money', money that you can lay your hands on and spend, but M4 requires a visit to the bank manager to arrange a special loan. The monetarist could therefore sit in his economic control tower and tell us if M0, M4 or even M3 or any other M was getting out of control. As the dials flashed danger signals, of too much money chasing too few goods, the monetarist could reach for the

Graph 4: Britain's 1988 Error – Money and Lending 1984-92

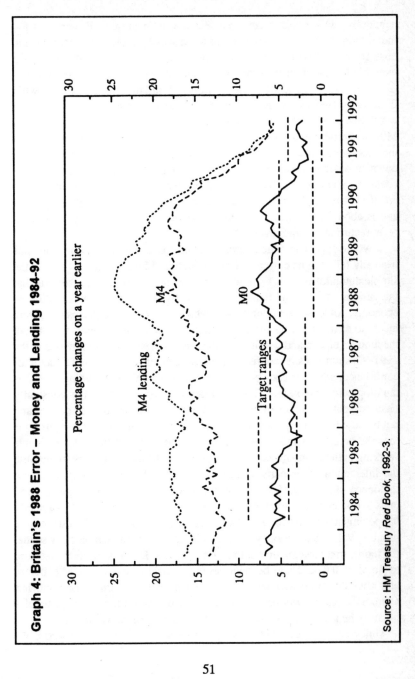

Percentage changes on a year earlier

M4 lending

M4

M0

Target ranges

1984   1985   1986   1987   1988   1989   1990   1991   1992

0   5   10   15   20   25   30

Source: HM Treasury *Red Book*, 1992-3.

handbrake, which was directly connected to interest rates. If there was too much money, all the monetarist had to do was to apply the handbrake and raise the cost of borrowing. As the cost of money itself rose, demand for it would fall off, as with any other commodity. As demand fell off, there would be less money in circulation and, hey presto!, inflation would be dealt with. In the early 1980s we were festooned with monetary signals every day of the week. In the early 1990s we hardly seem to hear about it. Nobody has got any M0 and everybody has got too much of the opposite of M4, namely debt, so the economy has stalled. The talk now is about the need to get interest rates down in order to create an economic recovery. The British Government's economic strategy in 1992 was to achieve zero inflation by high real interest rates! Unfortunately, however, unemployment is rising strongly as a result and is about to go through the three million level in Britain, yet again, as manufacturing declines even further.

It would appear that the approach of monetarism was too simple and has basically failed in its current state of evolution. Monetary targets are not the simple autopilot that we were led to believe they were. The problem is that the various M0 and M4 definitions interact with other variables within the economy, not least with interest rates which the monetarists themselves were meant to be determining and controlling. This is because interest rates affect the amount of demand within the economy, as is so painfully obvious in the 1991-92 slump. Demand itself is dependent on the intangible factor of confidence, which cannot be measured in any way. A definition of M? is tautologically impossible. The confidence factor refers to the constantly changing nature of human beings as it is driven by our 'feeling centre' and not by anything purely rational or remotely mathematical. The conclusion is that the economist must have an understanding of all the other elements working in the economy as well. For example, there is no attempt to measure the interaction of property values, availability of credit, employment and incidence of taxation. So the monetarist connects up yet more gauges and dials to obtain more and more data in an effort to understand what is actually happening in the real economy. Perhaps a new dial called M25 could measure property values and property loans within London's orbital motorway so that the monetarist remembered not to forget the first factor in production. More to the point, it would have been interesting to do the calculation of M25 before and after the motorway was built. The Chancellor, Norman Lamont, has announced that he will be looking at house prices in future – about time! – but does he know whether it were best that they went down or up?

Unfortunately the monetarists' recent track record has not been good. M0 let them down badly in early 1988, when it gave only a bare indication of the coming inflationary surge that was about to swamp the British economy (see Graph 4). The Chancellor, Nigel Lawson, actually reduced interest rates in May 1988, at the very moment when the M0 dial should have been telling him more clearly to put them up! Although the Federal Reserve had spotted the forthcoming downturn in America in 1987, the British Treasury completely failed to see the impending recession until spring 1991 and then consistently mistook false dawns as 'green shoots' of recovery. As usually happens when dials and gauges go wrong and a vehicle crashes, the monetary engineers are now in force tinkering with the equipment and trying to work out what went wrong and how to get it to work better next time.

New definitions of M0, M4 and other Ms will no doubt emerge from the wreckage. This seems unlikely to happen in the near future as the monetarists clash head-on with the Keynesian reflationary tinkerers, who can only see their way out of the slump by slashing interest rates and printing more money to finance massive projects aimed at reducing unemployment. In the ensuing battle it should be noted that the position in Britain is not helped by the fact that since 1945 it has been politicians who control the Bank of England. The linkage between politicians and interest rates is too close for comfort. The public sinks into a dismal gloom and Joe and Jane rightly say that no one understands what is going on. The sad fact is that it appears to be true, so the economists go back to their computer models once again in search of a magic wand in the form of new software solutions and definitions. A new model or theory emerges that seems to work for a time, but if it is not based on the fundamental principles of the real economy, on an analysis of the primary factors of production, it is bound to fail.

Corrupt data do not just emanate from the Treasury's computer and economic forecasters. They are alive and well on the factory shop-floor as well. Here Degenerate Persons have a useful little rule called 'the speed of the slowest worker'. In order to lever up pay rates the idea of piece-work payments was introduced in the 1960s. The worker would get X pence for producing Y widgets. A nice person from the Time and Motion office in a white coat (a symbol of management) would stand back, so as not to get sploshed with machine oil, with a stop-watch in hand, while poor old Joe and Jane in cloth cap and hairnet got their hands dirty and did the bloody work. The trick was that Joe and Jane took longer to do the job than anyone else, so everyone else got more pay as well but production remained static. The only things that went up were pay, inflation and foreign competitors' order books. As Joe and Jane rightly remarked to each other, with a knowing wink, it was all a case of A^2LOB^2 ('All a Load of Bloody Bollocks') and deliberate corruption of time standards. As management gradually woke up to what was happening on the far-distant shop-floor another not-so-nice person appeared in a brown coat (a symbol of the unions) called the Health and Safety Officer, who advised the nice man from the Time and Motion Office on how fast a job should be done to preserve health and why the whole business of working was inherently dangerous anyway. Production still remained static, but absenteeism, sickness pay, inflation, foreign competitors' order books and the safety standards budget went up!

Computers grapple with and analyse economic data. They are calculators, giant calculators, that are designed to handle massive data, making them invaluable for scientific and business data manipulation. They are governed by a simple rule, however, called 'GIGO', or 'Garbage In, Garbage Out'. A computer's efficiency is only as good as the data put into it, combined with the ability of its operating and application software to manage that data to produce correct results. Any error in the input data, just like the data collected by the nice man from the Time and Motion Office, is extrapolated throughout all the computer's subsequent calculations. GIGO can turn into an epidemic of falsehood. Each forecaster's computer model has its own bells and whistles, but the key equations of most models cover basic input data such as consumer spending and business investment to such policy variables as the supply of bank credit and government expenditure and actual variables that can be observed and, in theory, measured, such as imports and exports, unemployment and mortgage rates.

The trouble is that the computer's innate accuracy is badly affected by two 'garbage in' failures. First, it is unable to quantify the human confidence factor and its relationship to the other variables. This factor is therefore omitted altogether. Worse still, when consumer attitudes and business investment intentions change, existing computer-based economic models that proved reliable in the past are unable to predict future trends. Secondly, the measurement of these other variables themselves is only as good as the variety of methods used for collecting accurate data in the first place. The size and structure of the UK economy should make it easier and quicker to collect meaningful data than in most countries, in that there is a mostly literate population concentrated in a very small country with a small number of entry points for aircraft and ships, a highly developed property and retail market and a banking system that depends on about ten domestic banks, including only four London clearing banks, which are required to provide timely and accurate data to the Bank of England. The fact that the UK Treasury's computer model has consistently failed for over a decade even to predict changes in the overall direction of the economy in terms of up and down does not augur well for those countries, like America, where the collection points of data are spread over a vast country with long borders and hundreds of airports and harbours, with over 10,000 banks and 50,000 other financial institutions. And, to add to the confusion, the population is continually increasing through illegal immigration, which is a problem that continental EC is only just beginning to wake up to after its leaders decided to sign the Schengen Agreement in the early 1990s accepting the principle of immigration. Nevertheless, UK economic data are full of errors and omissions. For example, the trade figures showing monthly balances are continually adjusted to allow for the odd jumbo jet or supertanker and other 'visibles' that turn up missing. The public is not informed, however, about the mechanism of collection of data or the basis of calculation. And what about 'invisibles' too? Does the Treasury really get to hear about all of these? More to the point, do other nations calculate their current account transactions in the same way? Has anyone done an audit on the Treasury's figures, or on the German or Italian or Spanish figures for that matter? It is important, for example, because the Bundesbank manages its exchange rate policy on such data.

Joe and Jane are not a uniquely British phenonenom. Luigi and Spiro are up to exactly the same tricks in Europe. When the local EC assessor turns up to count the peach and olive trees as a necessary preliminary to filling in a rebate claim for agricultural subsidies, there are plenty of heated discussions about the extent of the cultivations, requiring refreshments to be served on most occasions. When the assessors' returns were sent into the European Commission's offices, however, Brussels began to note that the combined totals of the orchards and groves regularly came to more than the actual size of whole regions. Now the EC has had to charter survey aeroplanes to produce aerial maps and evidence to cut down on fraudulent claims under the Common Agricultural Policy, which are alleged to be running at 10% of the total budget.

There is another problem for the statistician too, and that is how to account for the missing data of the underground economy. These transactions involve drug trafficking, handling of stolen goods and moonlighting. The temptation to work for cash and avoid the clammy grip of the tax inspector appeals both to the worker and to the client. The former receives more and the latter pays less. Since 1980, the Conservative Government in Britain has reduced income tax from 98% to 40% and has thereby reduced the incentive to avoid this particular tax. On the other hand, it has raised value added tax from 8% to

17.5% and directly boosted moonlighting in such areas as construction, domestic chores, car repairs, agents' commissions and back-alley shops. The only thing that is certain is that the underground economy is growing strongly, fuelled by the relentless spread of drugs and the soaring level of fraud and burglaries. In Britain the 1991-92 slump has even developed two whole new industries. Antique garden furniture and statuary now disappear overnight and are exported with the same speed as stolen motor cars. More audaciously, thieves have taken to ramming financial service outlets with mechanical diggers used on building sites to uproot cash-laden automatic telling machines to make off with them, with poor old M0 about the only one offering chase. On Tuesday 15th September 1992 Associated Newspapers Limited ran a survey of all reported crime in Britain. There were 15,195 crimes by Degenerate Persons on that one day, including 1,969 house burglaries, 1,787 other burglaries, 2,819 thefts from cars, 1,677 thefts of vehicles, 2,817 other thefts, 328 cases of fraud, 74 cases of arson and 44 cases of drug trafficking. The theft insurance claims were estimated at £4.21 million, arson claims were estimated at £1.36 million and the total estimated direct cost was £6 million, excluding policing and other costs, or an annual level of £2 billion. In America the Joint Economic Committee of Congress estimated in December 1983 that GNP data could be understating the real economy by between 5% and 20%!

Even when truncated data do arrive in varying stages of corruption in Washington, the political system of this great loveable country, which freely mixes and confuses money with politics and favours, and grants conflicting powers to the President and to Congress, allows Degenerate Persons to manipulate the data into an acceptable form for public consumption. Discouraging data are played down or even suppressed. It is well known that during 1991 in the run-up to the Presidential elections in November 1992 Richard Darman, the Controller of the Budget, controlled not so much the budget as the publication of economic data, and in a highly selective way. These data, which should have been issued by the relevant statistical agencies in the normal way, were deliberately parleyed to the media by Degenerate Persons so as to gloss over the actual recession, which Americans were beginning to feel very acutely as 1991 progressed. Darman's censorship and timing strategy backfired badly, however, as it became increasingly apparent that President Bush himself was about the only American who was unaware of the depth of the recession, a fact which he openly admitted during the New Hampshire Primaries in January 1992. Darman, like Norman Lamont in No 11 Downing Street, was determined to clutch at any straw to demonstrate that the corner had been turned. Manna from heaven even appeared to him in the form of a monthly increase in the receipts of the budget-priced Howard Johnson's national chain of motor inns! He failed to realise, or did not want to admit, that Americans were responding to the severity of the recession by simply trading down. The trouble for Britain is that although political interference in the publication of statistics is not meant to be possible, the Treasury's forecasts have still proved more unreliable than the US Federal Reserve's. On 12 October 1992, however, the *Financial Times* reported that Norman Lamont instructed the Treasury in March to 'massage' the PSBR totals down by £42 billion for the five years ending 1996-97, a month before the General Election. The article quoted an unnamed source as saying 'Lots of people fiddle numbers but the Treasury does it in a particularly professional way', a strange use of the word 'professional'. Lamont denied the thrust of the article.

The data that are eventually published by Westminster and Washington are extensive. Unfortunately they fail even to analyse taxation receipts in a way which would inform on the incidence of taxation between the two primary factors of production, property and industry. It is hardly surprising that our economists cannot see the wood for the trees as they too suffer from acute GIGO deficiency syndrome. For example, statistics showing the level of inflation are actually published every month, but both economies are slumping and asset prices are deflating. The price of houses, land, consumer durables, clothing, motor cars, airline and bus fares, restaurant prices and many other luxuries are all deflating. About the only increasing cost is the cost of unemployment and of the services of lawyers and accountants! The public is told that inflation is down to under 4%, which is political good news. Actually, inflation is minus and in double digits too, which is economic good news for reasons that will be revealed, but not good political news. In Britain there is even a debate to remove mortgage interest rates from the inflation figures altogether. The supposed argument is that as interest rates rise the underlying or core inflation does not rise. Under the present UK system, mortgage rate increases automatically drop out of the statistics after twelve months, giving an artificial reduction. Yet inflation inevitably communicates into rising property values as soon as actual interest rates do decline, but property values are not included in the inflation calculations! How else could the 'Housing Index' have risen nearly twice as much as the 'All Items Except Housing' index between 1974 and 1991? As someone once truly said, 'There are three kinds of lie: lies, damned lies and statistics.' We must stay on our guard and allow the Creative Person within us to step back from all preconceptions. We must maintain a healthy bogey factor in our attitude in order to counter GIGO and the other falsehoods perpetrated by Degenerate Persons.

Corrupt attitudes are even more debilitating than corrupt data. The example of A^2LOB^2 and time corruption on the factory floor stems from a them-and-us attitude. In a typical British company the managers and white-collar workers share car parks and dining-rooms and arrive late, while the blue-collar workers have separate facilities and have to arrive early. The resentment and disincentive caused by such attitudes has cost Britain dear. The resentment turns into this type of question from the production worker who cannot relate the hours, pay and effort of his work to what the boss is, or is not, doing: 'Why do they get paid all that money just to jet off to Taiwan for three weeks to get the next bloody order, when all they're doing is visiting the flesh-pots?' The failure to communicate between management and work-force has also cost Britain dear. The Germans and Japanese discuss every decision with the workforce and middle managers and agree a common goal so that everyone knows the game plan and who the 'enemy' really are. The shop stewards act as management, managers dress like workers and eat in the same dining-room. Workers imitate the Japanese and they all share the same car park. The Japanese implants and transplants in Britain work exceptionally well and the workforce responds positively and productivity is good. The Nissan car plant in Sunderland is at the top of the world productivity league. It is only the attitude that has changed. So you can't blame the worker if the manager does not manage and does not lead by example. The worker was demotivated by old-style British management and became content to earn a sufficiency and no more. This proved fertile ground for the trade union demagogues. The British workers never really respected such leaders and saw through them with their eyes shut, but they were content to pocket any increase that came their way through the exertions of others, just like the landlords who took the community value without paying for it. Why not, especially when the bosses were putting up their pay to astronomical levels? Is anyone really worth more than £250,000 per annum, or more than £1,000 per working day? Wage restraint must start at the top. Otherwise people below become Mumpers – 'Give them an inch and they'll take a mile' – and the next thing you know is that the Average Bastard is the Average British Bastard and an endless stream of corrupt attitude begins to fester and damage the economy and production.

Then the worker's attitude festers again as he reads that some Above Average British Bastard in the City, or Greedsville, has written a letter to hundreds of public companies urging them to keep up their dividend payments in the recession. A well-respected fund manager in the City actually did this in 1991 and stated reasonable views to support this immoderate advice. What this Degenerate Person had overlooked, however, was that the view from Sweat Street was that it was just another dose of 'Look after the rich and sod the workers'. The damage done by such stories breaking in the tabloids puts another spin on pay-claims, inflation and lost production. What the advice should have been was quite the opposite: 'Keep your R&D, marketing efforts and training going for the future and only pay a dividend from free cash resources, having allowed for a safety margin.' It is all a question of the attitudes of Creative and Degenerate Persons.

Until the 1980s Creative Pesons in the City enjoyed a majority and 'my word is my bond' was the writ that ran large. The Greed Decade of the 1980s, however, nurtured the ultimate corrupt attitude of 'something for nothing'. Degenerate Persons misinterpreted Thatcherism as granting them licence to make a profit by any means as the ultimate end. Fraud and falsehood threatens the City's future, but it is hard to see how standards fell so quickly. The decline has run parallel with the decline in family attendance at church and a reduction in the number of religious services at schools and universities. In fact about the only thing that has declined further than British manufacturing industry has been attendance at Church of England services. Now we hear that Degenerate Persons at the Church Commissioners have lost £500 million in property speculation in America. Serves them right! Meanwhile, Sunday is being given over to money, as the City slicker backs horses, Joe does the pools and Jane goes to bingo. They all hope to win and get a return on a small outlay and now on Sunday too. The British love gambling, just like the Church Commissioners in the property market, and they love the fact that their houses seem to go up in value for no obvious reason and certainly without any effort. As they earn something for nothing asleep at night from rising house values, they go to work the next day and expect the same treatment there.

In the meantime the politicians and economists urge industrialists to work harder, invest more, hold back pay and costs and export or die, as though they had just majored at the University of Hard Rock Experience. The only thing that is clear is that practically no one actually knows what they are talking about in relation to the real economy. This engenders another corrupt attitude, which is starkly obvious: 'I've heard it, I can't take it and I can't stand it any more!' Joe and Jane sit in their lounge watching telly with the imported premium lager in their hand and shout back at the screen: 'We, the British People, have seen through the lie! You don't know what you're talking about!' They shout in unison, as yet another Mandarin in a pin-striped suit who has the standard Treasury we-know-best look on his face, and has carefully kept out of trade and business and production and all those sort of nasty things, expounds the latest Treasury appeal to moderate pay claims because M0 is overheating, along with other favourite A^2LOB^2 dicta.

'He's right, yer know Jane, I told you we did that last job too bloody quick!'

'Naw Joe, it's all right, 'cos Charlie in Stores fixed the bloody stop-watch anyway!'

And the whole absurd play goes on and the economy sinks into its now familiar routine of boom-bust decline, with unemployment, government debt, bank loan provisions and taxation all up and with manufacturing, government spending, congregations and confidence all down. The inevitable sterling crisis and devaluation just closes the chapter on another 'wasted' decade. Then the Prime Minister and Chancellor of the hour ritually adopt another corrupt attitude and say in unison 'It's all somebody else's fault! Speculators, foreigners, the Bundesbank or the unions!' The flip-side of this particular attitude is that 'It's all so unfair – boo-hoo!' Baloney!

6

The Primary Cause of Inflation and Unemployment

Everyone is agreed that inflation and unemployment are two of the worst economic evils that beset mankind, but it seems that no two economic schools of thought are agreed on how they are caused or how to deal effectively with them. It is quite extraordinary that this should be so. It is as if inflation and unemployment were two ghosts that are sent to haunt us but we are powerless to apprehend them and demand where they come from. 'That which is present cannot be denied' is an old rule, and there is no question that inflation and unemployment are definitely with us. But in our apparent inability to explain their cause and origins it is as though we are turned into gibbering ghosts ourselves and appear completely incapable of explaining or preventing their unwelcome presence in our midst. In the OECD capitalist countries alone unemployment in 1992 is nearly 7.5%, which amounts to thirty million workers – yes, 30,000,000!

The first natural law of economics is that everything in the man-made world comes from the earth and returns to her. Everything in the man-made world is created by the application of labour on land. This therefore appears to be a sensible point from which to track down the cause of these twin evils of inflation and unemployment. In our example of the tribe inflation did not arise, and no one ever heard of an unemployed tribe-person. In the communist system it is claimed that they do not to arise, except when President Yeltsin ordered prices to rise when he introduced a new currency value as part of his introduction of market prices in 1991. It is clear that capitalism, however, contains within its very structure the seed of an imbalance that distorts the natural relationship between property and industry. Capitalism is always co-existent with outright ownership of land which can be freely bought and sold like any other commodity. As the community expands, so the value of property goes up. As property goes up so does the price of property, as measured by rent. There is nothing wrong with this at all. In fact, it is an entirely natural and inevitable process that creates 'community value'.

The trouble starts when someone sells their land or house and, instead of buying another of the same size, buys a much smaller one and decides to go shopping instead with the rest of the money. Quite simply, the profit derived from the increase in the community value of this person's land or house is not matched by any production whatsoever as regards the increase in the land element. So, when this person cashes in the profit, more money is available to buy the fruits of production, but production is still at the same quantum level and so prices do go up. In fact this person did not even have to sell their house in the 1980s decade of instant credit in order to go shopping, because he or she could just as well have gone to the local bank or building society and borrowed money on the increasing property value. They could simply have kept the house and still gone shopping and, for example, bought a new car at the same time. In effect homeowners could drive around town in their newly mortgaged house extensions. True, they would now have a debt obligation, which would need servicing with interest payments. If everyone borrows heavily against the increased value of their house, however, thereby enlarging M4, and then they all go shopping at the same time, thereby enlarging M0, then prices will of necessity have to rise so as to divide the available production by the increased level of money now in circulation. If domestic production cannot meet the demand or produce the goods people want, imports go up, the balance of payments suffers, the value of sterling declines so that imports cost more and inflation rises. One way of reducing inflation in these circumstances is to increase domestic production. If interest rates rise, however, the cost of money rises which is itself inflationary, and production is choked at the same time as demand is held back. As is so evident in the 1991-92 recession, the whole system ends up fighting itself. This produces the worst of all worlds where the necessity is to bring down inflation during the short cycle recession rather than preventing it rising in the preceding boom (see Graph 5).

The uncomfortable thing about this absurdly simple illustration is that it is almost exactly what did happen during the booming 1980s. The real increase in British residential property values from 1969 to 1988, after allowing for inflation, rose two-and-a-half times. Between 1974 and 1991 the 'Housing Index' rose 857.1%, which was approaching double the index for 'All Items Except Housing', which rose 464% (source: *Retail Prices 1914-1990*, published by the CSO). As this increase in house prices was in excess of the continuing levels of inflation, this was actually setting up a store of 'unearned value', or a value not matched by any production, which would drive inflation and wages up and unleash more purchasing power when sold or borrowed on. Just to help the whole inflationary, debt-driven process, building societies circulated junk mail to their mortgagors in the 1980s

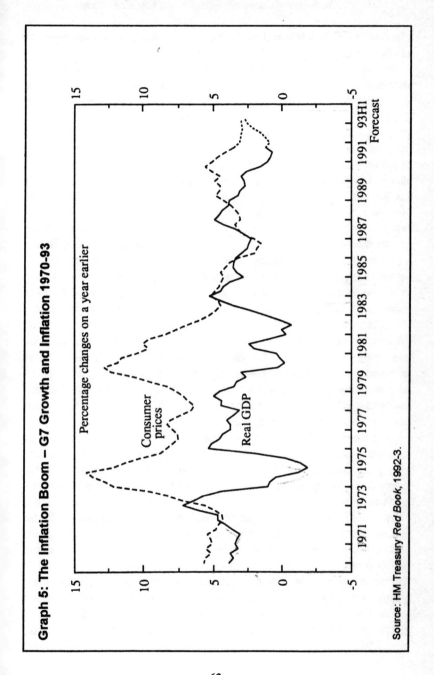

Graph 5: The Inflation Boom – G7 Growth and Inflation 1970-93

Percentage changes on a year earlier

Consumer prices

Real GDP

Source: HM Treasury *Red Book*, 1992-3.

63

offering foreign holidays and other frivolities, payable over the remaining life of the mortgage!

In the early 1990s the exact opposite is happening in that inflation is declining rapidly as property values fall, as a result of massive debts secured on properties. The simple fact is that under the present economic structure all expansion of the community communicates directly to land values. Once property values have gone up and a new level of prices for things generally is established they rarely go back down again to the previous levels. They could only go back down by deflation, which is a rare phenomenon. Debt-induced deflation in property values is actually occurring in 1991-92 for only the second time since WW2; the other time was briefly in 1974-75. The trouble is that, as property and other assets deflate, the reward to labour does not go down as workers from the Prime Minister and MPs down will not countenance a reduction in their hard-pressed compensation. In fact in Britain many of the larger pay deals include an inflation-proof element anyway, which is triggered by cost-of-living indices and takes no account of asset deflation. Parliamentary salaries were increased in 1992, just as deflation was setting in, which was an unfortunate message to send to the electorate. On 7th September 1992, for example, Vauxhall Motors, part of Detroit's General Motors, granted a pay rise of 4.2%, based on the 3.7% July official inflation rate, plus 0.5%, as part of a two-year deal. Consequently, as recovery eventually comes, the high relative salary and wage levels cause house prices to rise rapidly once again, as they catch up to their historic average of around two-and-a-half times earnings, and the stage is then set for the whole miserable process to begin all over again.

The commercial property market also contains some distinct inflationary characteristics of its own. In Britain, in particular, as we have seen, commercial leases contain 'upwards only' rent revision clauses which are triggered every five years or so. In fact the rent is automatically reset at a higher level and cannot be reset at a lower level. To the extent that rent increases exceed the level of inflation since the previous increase, they are inflationary. To the extent that rents decrease as a result of deflation, existing rentals are not reduced as the terms of the leases prevent any reduction. That too is inflationary, just like inflation-proof pay rises. To take an actual example, a major British company entered into a standard 25-year lease in 1989, with five yearly 'upwards only' rent reviews, paying £10.30 per square foot for provincial office space some fifty miles north of London. In 1992 it vacated the building, but it is still contractually bound to keep paying the rent for the next 22 years. Its agents have put the premises on the market and it is seeking sub-tenants at around £8 per square foot. The market from 1989 to 1992 therefore fell by 20% or more. At the first rent review in 1994 the rent will probably not have risen back to the passing rent of £10.30 per square foot, but the company that signed the lease must continue paying at this inflated price all the same. Just as the worker is loth to see a reduction in wages, so the commercial landlord protects existing rental levels. The landlord is normally in a stronger position than the worker, however, as economic expansion reflects into increasing property values as an automatic process. In the 1991-92 recession, however, the landlord with a building but no tenant was caught in the deflationary cycle as well. Many such landlords therefore kept empty property off the market with the deliberate intention of waiting until rents recovered. This too is inflationary, as premises that could have been let out at lower rentals were kept out of economic use. Some Degenerate Person landlords even deliberately vandalised whole buildings so that they could avoid paying the uniform business rate altogether, which negative cost factor was the only real incentive to let the premises at the current market price.

The second primary factor of production, namely labour, can also cause inflation in other ways. It is widely appreciated that pay settlements in excess of productivity must be inflationary. The 'wildcat' strikes of Degenerate Persons in the 1960s and 1970s clearly caused inflation, particularly in Britain, as production was severely disrupted and the level of pay settlements actually bankrupted large tracts of industry, such as the car industry. What was not so widely perceived by Creative Persons was that pay rises quickly fed through into increased property values as well, in a vicious circle. The damage caused by strikes was obvious and polarised the discussion on inflation around the need to curb excessive pay settlements. The damage caused by increasing property values in real terms was not so obvious and has hardly ever been publicly discussed. Legislation in the 1980s has broken the monopoly power wielded by trade unions over labour. Legislation or fiscal corrective action is clearly needed to curb the land monopoly, as well as the banks' excessive lending secured on property. For the eighth principle of economics is that increases in property values indirectly create purchasing power beyond production and an asset value that demands more rent from production.

If the source of inflation lies at the third point where labour meets land it seems probable that the roots of unemployment may well lie there too. Once again, no one has ever heard of a tribe which suffered from unemployment, although starvation from forces outside their control was always a threat. In the communist system of the former USSR the Soviets loved to proclaim they had no unemployment either, although they overlooked the fact that there was not too much actual employment, or rather work, for those in apparent employment, other than in their successful sectors such as aerospace and metallurgy-based industries. But in our capitalist system unemployment has become a part of the landscape. It is not as though everyone has got everything they need and so there is no need to work. On the contrary, there is alarming poverty, homelessness and even under-nourishment. In America the inner urban blight is a problem which will threaten the social cohesion of the whole country unless there is a visible improvement in the environment and in the standard of living of the inhabitants. The situation in certain British cities is not much better, as several recent urban riots have testified. What is particularly frustrating in the capitalist system is the sight of an unemployed person doing nothing when there is work crying out to be done. In Britain in 1992 unemployment is greatest in the construction sector, and yet the public is told that many classrooms and wards in the nation's schools and hospitals are in urgent need of repair. There is clearly something basically wrong. The need is there and the labour is available and something keeps them apart. The answer that the schools and hospitals do not have the money is merely to state the obvious. Why don't they have the money? In the capitalist competitive market free-for-all, the school and hospital repair bills have lost out to other claims on resources. In fact, the resources tied up in the property markets have to that extent competed successfully against other claims. What has been invested and lent out on land cannot also be invested or lent out elsewhere. To the extent that these resources were invested in the actual construction of buildings they did of course provide employment. But the cost element that went into the undeveloped site to purchase what was really the community value did no such thing.

As the community value of an economy's property rises, labour must pay a higher rent to gain access to property or land on which to work. Like any other cost of production, such as wages and taxation, the higher the costs rise, the more industry is squeezed. An actual example of a British engineering firm that went bust in the 1991 downturn will show the effect of this. The company operated from its own freehold premises which it had acquired many years previously for £600,000. The company's actual sales were £10,000,000 and its net profit after tax was £500,000. This looked a reasonable level of profits, but in fact the ownership of the freehold meant that the company did not pay an economic rent. The company became insolvent as it had guaranteed its parent company's bank overdraft to make an over-priced

66

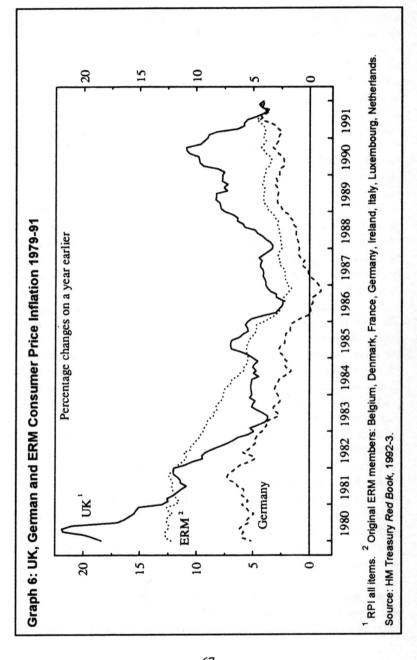

Graph 6: UK, German and ERM Consumer Price Inflation 1979-91

Percentage changes on a year earlier

UK[1]

ERM[2]

Germany

1980 1981 1982 1983 1984 1985 1986 1987 1988 1989 1990 1991

[1] RPI all items. [2] Original ERM members: Belgium, Denmark, France, Germany, Ireland, Italy, Luxembourg, Netherlands.

Source: HM Treasury *Red Book*, 1992-3.

acquisition in America. Unfortunately the value of its freehold factory property had risen over the years by ten times to £6,000,000. The problem for any would-be buyer of the business assets was that the cost of funding the freehold factory, which was completely surrounded by housing, would have more than wiped out the profit on manufacturing. The rise in the value of the factory had effectively made the operation an economic failure. If the company had not owned its own freehold but had paid rent instead it would have gone bankrupt several years previously. Alternatively if the management had not enjoyed the cushion that the freehold ownership had provided, they would have been forced to run the operation more efficiently and to pay the economic rent in the meantime. Efficient industries should pay the economic rent created by the expansion of the community and the infrastructure provided by it. What is also clear, though, is that in a capitalist system the property market competes with the labour market. The ninth principle of economics is that the higher property values rise, the more marginal industry becomes. Or, to push the argument to its absurd limit, if the price of property could be infinite no industry could afford to pay the rental and everyone would be unemployed.

Secondary factors driving property values and markets do not help either. The massive credit tied up in funding property also raises the cost of borrowing for industry. When unemployment itself goes up in the downturn, the social welfare costs fall mainly on industry, as property only employs a minor proportion of the workforce except during actual construction. In Britain an unemployed worker will have his mortgage payments – no less! – paid by the government for six months from yet more taxes on industry or from borrowings. And when a property development collapses the banks that financed it seem to charge their other customers by fair means and foul to recover their losses.

Luckily there is an economic model on display which has resisted the Anglo-American obsession with property ownership. In West Germany, ever since the Great Inflation of 1923, banks invest in and lend to industry as their main function in the economy and look to the long-term benefit. Before unification with East Germany in 1990 inflation in West Germany bumped along at an average 2%. Even after the second oil crisis in 1979 West Germany's inflation only reached an unacceptable 5% compared with Britain's horrendous 22% (see Graph 6). Moreover West Germany's unemployment has consistently been lower than Britain's jobless total. The structural difference between the British and German economies reflects partly on national traits of character, but mainly on a different approach to the tax structure of local government as it affects property values and their funding. (This will be examined further in Chapter 7.)

During the long cycle's downswing, it is unlikely that major companies will be recruiting on a big scale. It is far more likely that they will be shedding labour instead, as witnessed by recent redundancies in the banking, car, aerospace and construction industries. New employment generated by out-of-town shopping centre developments has only a limited scope. There will be reduced employment prospects in central and local government too, as well as in the former state utilities. There is only one sector which can really create new jobs, namely the Small and Medium-sized Enterprises, or SMEs, to give them their cacophonic EC definition. In fact SMEs form a much greater part of the structure of the Continental European economies than is generally realised. After the devastation of WW2 industry revived with the creation of thousands of family businesses, which today typically have revenues of a few hundred thousand pounds to thirty and fifty millions. The enterprise culture was revived by Mrs Thatcher and the British venture capital industry came of age in the 1980s. The recession of 1991-92 has set back the process. Even within this revival more emphasis needs to be on real invest-ment in new enterprises or genuine development capital for existing busi-nesses than on HLTs and MBOs. The introduction of the Business Expansion Scheme (BES) in 1985 as a tax-shielding investment scheme, designed by Creative Persons to enable individuals to invest up to £40,000 per annum in smaller companies with growth potential, was derailed by Degenerate Per-sons who bent the rules and invested in farms, wine cellars, yachts and property instead. It was a pity, as Britain cannot generate too many SMEs for her own good.

In the inflationary double spiral of rising wages and property prices, it seems in retrospect that organised labour, led by irresponsible trade union leaders who were not answerable to anyone outside their own constituency, led the inflation charge in the 1960s through to the first major miners' strike in 1975. From then on property prices increased, driven by bank lending, and took up the running on inflation through to the 1990s. Natural market forces are now sending the nation a clear message. There is an imbalance in the economy that is destroying both jobs and property values in the world recession of 1991-93. Seen aright, this is a time for opportunity rather than dejection. The opportunity is to restructure the incidence of taxation to ensure that price inflation in wages and properties are both kept under control. The government believes membership of the ERM and the EC will achieve this. It will not, or cannot, under the present regime of fiscal imbalance.

6. The Primary Cause of Inflation and Unemployment

When the full negative impact of property on industry is looked at squarely, when the dreadful cost of inflation caused by surging property markets driven by credit booms and resulting in frequent banking crises, high real interest rates, ever higher wage demands and large-scale unemployment is all taken into account in each short-term cycle, the sane observer must question the whole process. The post-WW2 boom-bust cycles have destroyed large tracts of industry in Britain (and America too) and left millions in debt and without work. The human cost is enormous, but the issue now, as the long cycle turns down, is whether the UK economy can continue to operate in this way.

Insert 2

Who Needs the Treasury Computer? – Part One

'Last month this column warned of the MBO market turning down, and the dog days of August revealed the first serious cracks in recent deals; the first bubble to burst would appear to be the furniture/retail sector, which is usually the first to feel a pinch in the downward cycle. The walking wounded include Seaman Furniture Inc. in the US and MFI and Lowndes Queensway in the UK. Whereas Seaman (and SCI Television) are unlikely to cause sizeable problems, MFI represents the UK's largest MBO and already an extra £35 million needs to be injected.

'The problem in the UK is that no-one knows how far south this particular 'blip' will go. There is no let-up in sight for Sterling and UK interest rates will probably not decline significantly until 1992; the retail trade is set to plunge further... and at some point in the downward curve, senior debt will begin to control the equity. As other sectors begin to follow the furniture/retail sector down, opportunities for new investors to provide management buy-in and recovery funds on competitive terms will possibly become the vogue.'

Source: *Newsletter for Select Industries Trust*, September 1989.

Footnote: These predictions were made sixteen months before the White House acknowledged the recession. The UK Treasury was not much better: the Chancellor had just said that the downturn was only 'an economic blip'!

The Importance of the Incidence of Taxation

In a capitalist system, where land and labour are treated just like any other commodity or resource in the marketplace, these two primary factors interact on each other in various ways. The most crucial human decision at the third point where they meet is unquestionably the issue of taxation. This is because every form of tax ultimately can only fall either on property or industry, or on a combination of the two. In days gone by some republican parliamentarians decided to put a tax on chalk powder for wigs. This was clearly an indirect tax on the wig industry and had the effect of increasing the running costs of wearing a wig. This in fact was exactly what Oliver Cromwell intended. People would be discouraged from wearing wigs, which was taken as a pro-monarchist symbol! It was clearly a tax on production and was not a tax on property. On the other hand, the Mother of Parliaments did actually decide to put a tax on property. The yardstick adopted was, unfortunately and rather unintelligently, the number of windows in a residence. This was clearly an attempt to tax the value of property, but it backfired unexpectedly when householders decided to brick up their windows and thus reduce the amount of window-tax payable. Unfortunately some of the taxes introduced in Britain since WW2 have been almost as ill-conceived. For example, the Selective Employment Tax introduced in the 1970s, which was a payroll tax for service industries as opposed to manufacturing industries, had the opposite effect of what was intended. The tax was conceived by Degenerate Persons as an idea to boost employment in manufacturing. Its only effect was to reduce employment in service industries and so reduce employment overall. More recently, in the midst of the worst recession in the motor-car industry since WW2, the British government doubled the tax on new motor cars, helping to plunge the whole industry into an even greater crisis with the loss of 70,000 jobs from 1990-92. After this increase, the total tax on a car in Britain in 1992 was over 27%, compared with 14% in Germany and 19% in both France and Italy. Both these more recent taxes were taxes on labour and production rather than on property.

In the fiscal year 1991-92 the following amounts were budgeted to be raised by Her Majesty's Government, as set out in Table 2. The left-hand column, headed 'Receipts', shows the government's income from taxation, whereas the right-hand column, headed 'Expenditure', shows how it is spent.

A cursory glance at Table 2 reveals that there is no single dedicated tax on property values other than 'Rates', which relates to national non-domestic rates and local authority rates. There is, however, one classification of income tax which falls on rent which is not shown separately. Capital gains tax is also payable on the profit on a sale of property. However, this tax will only raise £1.4 billion in total in 1992-93, and tax advisers are very adept at avoiding it for their clients. Residential property taxes in Britain are raised by local government and not by central government. Local government pays for such expenditures as education, social services, law courts, police, fire services, refuse collection, street lighting and local roads and their maintenance. The tax on local residences in England and Wales was local authority rates until 1990 (Scotland – 1989), which were meant to be raised on the improved value of houses: that is, on the site value together with the actual construction, together referred to as the 'improved site value'. Rates, however, had lost touch with real values and were replaced by Mrs Thatcher's community charge in 1990-91, which was a poll tax on the adult headcount in each dwelling. The community charge, a euphemism for a poll tax, is being replaced by a new council tax in 1993, which will be raised on much the same principles as the former local authority rates: namely, as a proportion of the apparent value of houses in 1989, before deflation. The local tax on business premises is now known as the uniform business rate, as it is charged at the same rate of just under 41% of the former rateable value. Significantly all these local taxes only pay for about a fifth of local government costs, including education. The unfunded balance of local government expenditure is funded by way of support grant from the central government: that is, from the various taxes set out in Table 2. This 'Central Government Support for Local Authorities' is shown in Table 2 at £52.5 billion for 1991-92, which compares with total local authority expenditure originally estimated at £63.4 billion. Here is a major anomaly. The calculated value of all property in Great Britain at 31 December 1987 was a staggering sum, as shown in Table 3.

Table 2: Britain's 1991-92 Budget

£0,000,000,000s (billions)

Receipts		Expenditure		
Inland Revenue:		**Central Government Expenditure**		
Income tax	59.6	of which:	Social Security	58.3
Corporation tax	19.5		Health and OPCS	24.9
Capital gains tax	1.4		Defence	22.8
Inheritance tax	1.3		Scotland	5.8
Stamp duties	2.1		Wales	2.5
			Northern Ireland	6.4
			Other Departments	31.5
Total Inland Revenue	**83.9**			
		Central Government Support		
Customs & Excise:		**for Local Authorities**		**52.5**
Value added tax	35.7			
Petrol, duties etc	10.9	**Financing Requirements of**		
Tobacco duties	6.1	**Nationalised Industries**		**2.3**
Alcohol duties	5.2			
Betting & gaming	1.1	**Privatisation Proceeds**		**-5.5**
Car tax	1.3	**Reserve**		**3.5**
Customs duties	1.7			
Agricultural levies	0.2			
		Planning Total		**205.0**

Oil royalties	0.5	Central Government debt interest	16.7
Rates (local taxes)	14.4		
Other taxes & royalties	3.6*	Accounting adjustments	4.0*
Total Tax and Royalty Receipts	**167.6**		
Social security receipts	36.7**		
Community charge receipts	7.6		
Interest and dividends	6.1		
Trading surpluses and rent	3.3		
Other receipts	5.2*		
General Government Receipts	**226.5**	**General Government Expenditure**	234.8
Difference, being the Public Sector Borrowing Requirement (PSBR) (less Public Corp. Borrowing)	8.3		
	£234.8		

*   rounding amended so as to be additive at totals
**   formerly National Insurance Contributions
***   difference between total local expenditure and central government support

Source: *Financial Statement and Budget Report, 1992-93*, published by HM Treasury (the *Red Book*)

Table 3: Britain's Property Values in 1987

	£
Residential buildings	830,300,000,000
Agricultural land, buildings & forestry	35,700,000,000
Commercial buildings	222,200,000,000
Industrial buildings	27,600,000,000
	£1,115,800,000,000

Source: *U.K. National Accounts*, 1991 edition, published by the CSO (the *Blue Book*).

It is surprising to note that industrial buildings accounted for only 2.5% and agricultural premises for only 3.2% of the total. The total value of residential housing is an unbelievable £830.3 billion, representing 75% of the total. English people's homes really are their castles, but at what cost? The total for all properties at that date of £1,115.8 billion is more than two-and-a-half times the stock market value of Britain's FT-SE 100 capitalisation, which was around £400 billion at that date. Even if the value of all quoted companies on The International Stock Exchange, London was taken as amounting to £500 billion, with a 40% reduction of £200 billion for overseas operations, the value of UK properties is nearly four times as much as the market value of UK-based quoted industrial, commercial, banking and property operations taken together. The direct taxes on these property values, however, only pay for about 20% of local government expenditure and possibly 3% of central government expenditure, before taking into account the distortionary effects of mortgage interest tax relief, despite the fact that these expenditures are in the main related to maintaining the serviceability of the communal infrastructure and are therefore related to the general value of properties.

There is an important relationship between property values (and therefore the rents that property commands) and the level of taxation levied on the capital or annual value of property. The cost of occupation of a building, whether for business or residential purposes, comprises mainly rent for business premises and mortgage repayments for residences, together with local taxes. (We can leave aside the other running costs such as insurance, lighting and heating, as they are for actual services rendered.) The businessman or householder looks at the sum of these two major outgoings, rent or interest plus local taxes, and then determines the affordability of a particular property. If the taxes on a property are high, the prospective tenant will only be prepared to pay a lower rental or mortgage repayment, as he or she is not prepared or able to pay a higher sum and the local taxes as well. In effect the rental value of a property is reduced if local taxes are increased. Rent is in effect the sponge which soaks up the difference between what the market can stand as a total occupancy cost, less the amount of local taxes. If the taxes go down, the rent will go up, and vice versa. If the rent rises, the capital value also rises.

There is nothing obscure about this close tango between rent and rates. In the Great Depression of the late 1920s and early 1930s, when unemployment reached over 15% of the British workforce and when the landed gentry of Britain were a most powerful lobby at Westminster, the latter campaigned for the removal of local taxes on agricultural land, in order to ease the effects of the downturn for the farming community. They got their way, and in 1929 the Agricultural De-Rating Act was passed. The final quarter of local authority rates or local taxes were removed from agricultural land altogether for the direct benefit of farmers. Unfortunately the tenant farmers did not enjoy this saving as the rents they were charged by their landlords promptly increased by the amount that they had been relieved of the local rates. The removal of tax simply meant that rents increased for the tenant farmers to soak up the tax giveaway. After the first De-Rating Act of 1896, which removed one half of local rates on agricultural land, Thomas Usborne, Conservative MP for Chelmsford, said candidly: 'No one has denied, and I hope no one wishes to deny, that the [Agricultural De-] Rating Act was in relief of the landlord and not the tenant.' So there you have it, beyond denial.

In order to arrive at some appreciation, however rough and ready, of how much taxation actually falls on land or properties and how much on labour or industry, it is necessary to take each major tax and attempt to assess its incidence on the two primary factors of production. The biggest amount of revenue in Britain (and America) is raised on payroll taxes deducted by employers from employees' salaries and wages. Such payroll deductions in Britain comprise most of the income tax and all the social security receipts set out in Table 2. In both America and Britain there persists a great myth concerning the nature of payroll taxes, which is that such taxes are paid by employees as a tax on their earnings, apart from employers' so-called contributions as defined. This view is a myth because the taxes are actually paid over by the employers and are in effect a tax on employment. True, the amount actually paid by the employer, ostensibly on behalf of the employee, is calculated by a reference to each employee's personal details, both as regards each employee's earnings and the allowable deductions in relation to each employee's financial and social circumstances. The working employee, however, whether on a monthly salary or a weekly wage, is only interested in the net pay that he or she will receive after payroll deductions have been made. (There are other payroll deductions besides tax – for example, the cost of national and/or private medical insurance – but I am only talking of actual taxes deductible from the payroll.) When an employer offers a prospective employee £25,000 for a year's work, the would-be employee does a rapid mental calculation to reduce the gross compensation to the actual net pay receivable, or 'take-home pay'. This calculation is practically always linked to the minimum would-be employees will accept, bearing in mind the nature of the job and the outgoings to maintain their accepted standard of living. They tend to seek only that level of sufficiency. The fact is that the employer is commissioned by the government with calculating and deducting payroll taxes and the employer actually pays the government the amount of tax deducted. The aggregate of payroll taxes is treated as a cost to the employer and, when added to the aggregate net take-home pay of all employees, represents the labour cost of producing a manufacture or of providing a service, and is duly treated as an expense in the employer's annual profit and loss account. Payroll taxes look like taxes on employees, but in actual fact are taxes on employers. Therefore payroll taxes are a tax on industry. This impact is obvious when the opportunity for overtime occurs. The worker has already achieved his or her sufficiency level and is not incentivised to work more hours and be taxed at the higher rate of income tax, so production does not keep pace with demand and the supply side of the economy falters, sucking in more imports. Overtime should be deemed to start after a nationally agreed standard working week has been worked and be taxed at the lower rate of income tax, thereby encouraging domestic production.

The conclusive evidence that payroll taxes are indeed a tax on industry is that the tax inspector accepts the deduction of these costs, 'incurred wholly, exclusively and necessarily in the conduct of the company's business or trade', as being tax-deductible expenses themselves in determining the employers' liability to pay taxes on their profits. The main British payroll tax is 'income tax' which, rather confusingly, is also charged on rental income in the hands of individuals, which in this context is a property-based tax. The amount of income tax raised each year by the British government is not analysed in the Budget Statement (or *Red Book*) between payroll taxes and rental taxes, but the former represents by far the greater proportion of the total. In fact, the *Red Book* does not analyse income tax on earnings as distinct

7. The Importance of the Incidence of Taxation

from rental income. The National Accounts, or *Blue Book*, however, states that income tax on salaries and wages in 1990 amounted to £49 billion and on 'dividends, interest, rent and trading income [of sole traders, partnerships and other unincorporated entities]' amounted to £11.2 billion. It can be inferred therefore that income tax on property rentals could only approximate to around 10% of the total of income tax at most. The *Blue Book* also gives a break-down for 1990s 'Social Security contributions', between employers (£20.1 billion), employees (£13.5 billion) and the self-employed (£1.2 billion). In fact the total of this tax of £34.8 billion is borne by and paid over by employers as well, as it is a payroll deduction tax, just like income tax. The distinction between what is paid by employees and employers is simply slavishly following the way the tax regulations are drafted rather than reflecting economic reality. As with income tax paid over by employers ostensibly on behalf of employees, it is also a tax which falls on employers and is also accounted for by them as a cost of production in their annual profit and loss account, both for the employees' 'contribution' and the employers' actual contribution. And the tax inspector also allows both parties' contributions to be deducted from the employers' profits for tax purposes, under the provisions for corporation tax. The truth is that payroll taxes are employment taxes.

The next most significant tax is value added tax ('VAT'). This tax operates throughout Europe and is equivalent to sales tax in America. US sales tax is charged at the point of sale to the customer, whereas VAT is a cascade tax that is payable and recoverable at every stage of the production process. This means the net tax is receivable at an earlier stage in the production process. (It also provides useful statistical data about different industries and sectors.) Essentially both these taxes are a tax on the final consumer and are received on behalf of the government at the point of sale by the retailer. These taxes are not a tax either solely on industry or solely on property. Rather confusingly, they are a tax on both. A tax on a finished product increases the price of the product. Some of that increase must be a drag on production, because it makes the finished article more expensive. The rest of the increase must be a tax on the rental value of the retail outlet. A shop on Oxford Street will sell more widgets to consumers than a 'Mom & Pop' shop in Little Blissington-on-the-Marshes. On a sales per square footage basis, the stores in London will sell far more widgets per square foot than their country cousins. They will collect and pay over far more VAT to the authorities. If the major city sites command far higher rentals, it is clear that the greater quantum of VAT raised on these sites must partly be a disguised property tax. This is because the better site is better precisely because it generates greater sales and therefore more VAT. What is not at all clear, however, is how much of the VAT is an indirect tax on industry or an indirect tax on property rentals. This is one of the beauties of such taxes from the point of view of governments, as it confuses this important issue very effectively, thus reducing the usual opposition lobbies. What is clear is that these taxes are a tax on consumption, and so the fragmented body of consumers is the only effective opposition to them, despite the fact that they must be a drag on both industrial production and property rentals.

Taxes on imported raw materials, on fuels and on finished manufactures such as motor cars, and on alcohol and tobacco, fall solely or mainly on production. Taxes payable on death fall entirely on the estates of private individuals, and I suspect that in property-owning democracies they fall mainly on property, but in any event such taxes are hardly significant in the context of the total tax-take. Alcohol and tobacco duties, which are similar in some ways to taxes on betting, are effectively taxes on legalised drug industries. These duties tend to represent a high proportion of the selling price of these products, which are remarkably resilient in terms of sales to the ever-increasing duties imposed on them. Would consumers, one wonders, drink twice as much whisky if the price was halved? I suspect that sales would not rise in direct proportion to any price reduction, as people who do drink whisky seem to drink about the same amount regardless of cost, which is usually more than is good for them. Penniless drunkards seem to have a remarkable knack of procuring the cash for their next necessary fix regardless of price, as does the 'hundred-a-day' smoker of cancer sticks. True, if one shop offered these substances at half the price of another shop, we all know which shop would get the business. But would their sales achieve double the volume at half-price? It seems unlikely. Nevertheless there must be an element of rental drag in such taxes in terms of reduced sales. Actual sales would be somewhat higher if overall prices were lower, so production suffers too. It is hard to determine a view on how much of such taxes falls on land and how much on labour, but it feels like a case of six of one and half-a-dozen of the other. The tax gatherer's conscience is easy over the issue either way, as these taxes are 'social cohesion taxes' as well. Leaving aside the moral arguments, if only soft drugs like cannabis were legalised, just think of the tax revenue that could be derived! The higher the tax, however, the less would be sold. The trick, from a purely fiscal standpoint, is not to over-tax these particular geese that lay such golden tax eggs, but to balance the addictive power of the drug with what the market will pay for the addiction.

7. The Importance of the Incidence of Taxation

Finally, local rates and their temporary surrogate, community charge, and their planned replacement, council tax, create special problems in determining their incidence. (I shall assume that community charge is levied on the same basis as local authority rates for the present purpose, as there seems little point in discussing the alleged merits and demerits of the redundant poll tax, apart from observing that the only other country with a form of poll tax is Papua New Guinea!) Local rates and the new council tax are meant to be levied on the value of houses. They are therefore in theory levied on both the site or community value and on the completed property. If the property is extended, the value goes up and so does the tax on it. Therefore a proportion of the tax is levied on labour or industry, in fact on the actual building itself. The greater proportion actually falls on the site value regardless of the building, but an improvement or new extension puts up the value and therefore the local tax or rates, and some of the tax must therefore fall on production and not on land. In practice, rating valuations tended to trail market values, reducing the yield from these taxes. It should be noted that the term 'rate' means the number of pence in the pound of the somewhat arbitrary 'valuations' that are actually payable, so the actual yield from old-style rates was probably well below the actual annual 'community value' or economic rent of the bare site, even excluding the building element. In fact one of Mrs Thatcher's justifications for the introduction of the disastrous community charge was that rating values had fallen so out of line with the real market that it would cost too much to produce a new general valuation. That, however, is exactly what the market itself actually does, and at no cost.

It should now be possible to make a very approximate and arbitrary analysis between the total quantum of taxation that appears to fall on industry and the total amount that would appear to fall on property. Such an analysis will probably not be accurate to within plus or minus several percentage points as there is clearly a very wide area for argument either way. What is quite clear is that the greater part of taxation in Britain (and America) is borne by industry and is disproportionate to underlying property values. That this imbalance in the incidence of taxation favours property rather than industry is borne out by the massive values tied up in property, both developed and undeveloped. It is true that in the slump of 1991-92 property values have fallen significantly, but this phenomenon is mainly accounted for by the excessive debt levels secured on property and the fact that the supply of certain types of buildings, especially offices, vastly exceeds demand as a consequence.

In fact industry suffers from a double whammy from this collapse in property values in a way which is not so obvious. As the banks are forced to make massive write-downs on their property loan portfolios, they are allowed to write off these losses for tax purposes against profits derived from their corporate and personal clients and from their credit card operations, which often charge interest rates of over 30% per annum. Just as the bankers' good loans pay for their bad loans, so the government pays the first loss on the banks' property loan losses by the amount of the current rate of taxation on corporate profits, which is currently 35% in Britain (and 34% in America). In effect the first third or so of the banks' property loan losses are paid for by the government. The only money any government has, however, is raised from borrowing or from taxation, which as we have seen falls mainly on industry. In fact, industry therefore pays for the first slug of bad loans incurred by banks in the property market as well. In order to appreciate something of the size of the disproportionate incidence of taxation between what have been simply termed property and industry in the British economy, Table 4 attempts to reformat the receipts side of Britain's 1991-92 Budget set out in Table 2, analysed on a 'best guess' basis to indicate the general incidence of taxation between the two primary factors of production.

The conclusion of this very arbitrary analysis indicates that the taxes levied on production are about three times more in total than on property. Property, whose market value in Britain is approximately four times or more than the stock market value of quoted UK productive assets, only bears about a quarter of the tax burden. In fact it is not quite as simple as that, because Table 3 showed that 75% of the property values of Britain were represented by domestic residences, which are nothing directly to do with production. However arbitrary the reckoning is behind Table 4 – and it is very arbitrary as the government's figures fail to take into account the incidence of taxation on the two primary factors of production, take note! – an important fact is clear and beyond dispute. In Britain (and in America too), the greater part of the tax burden, about three-quarters, falls on the shoulders of industry and the greatest beneficiary is the residential housing market, which bears relatively little tax, indeed not even enough to pay for its own direct servicing costs. In fact the figures in Table 2 even omit to mention the annual cost to the Treasury of mortgage interest relief on residences, as it is in effect deducted from income tax receipts. The current tax allowance on mortgage interest is on the first £30,000 of a householder's mortgage and 'costs' the British taxpayer £6.1 billion per annum in lost revenue, which approximates to the total income tax take on rents! In the 1950s the cost of this relief in constant terms was only several hundred millions. In short, we are taxing industry rather than property. We are penalising actual effort and production and effortlessly creating property value instead. No wonder we have created a property-owning democracy which treats work as a four-letter 'K-word'! As I and no doubt many of you now mature readers realised in the early 1970s property boom, why get up in the morning to go to work to be taxed when you can make more, tax-free, as a Degenerate Person staying in bed.

The situation in Continental Europe is quite different, especially as regards taxation to cover local government costs. The continentals raise local taxes to fund practically all local expenditure. Denmark, Italy, France and Germany have local land or income taxes or ground rents. Moreover, the proportion of home ownership is much less than in Britain. West Germans tend to rent their homes during the first two decades of their working life and then 'self-build' houses from their savings. They are required to deposit 25% for a new dwelling and pay off their mortgage within ten years. This regime keeps a lid on prices. In Britain, deposits may be nil to 10%, with up to twenty-five years or more to pay off the mortgage. This lax regime takes the lid off prices. Only 40% of West Germans own their own homes, compared with 67% in Britain, according to Germany's embassy in London. (Interestingly enough the embassy said the percentage had hardly changed in the 1980s, although other sources claim the total in Germany is higher at 47%.) This was not always the case in Britain. At the turn of the century owning your own house was not considered essential or even ideal, and in Scotland this is still the prevailing view. In 1914 90% of Britain's houses were privately rented, compared with 7% in 1992. Between WW1 and WW2, the percentage level of home ownership, the price of property generally, wages and retail prices all stayed remarkably constant in Britain, before, after and during the Great Depression. By 1953 home ownership in Britain had risen from 10% to 29%, passing the 50% mark around 1970 on its way to the current 67% peak. It was no coincidence that the spurt in home ownership from the 1960s coincided with three decades of debilitating inflation in Britain.

In West Germany, by contrast, all taxes payable by individuals are paid to the regional state, or *Land* (pronounced *Lunt*). The *Land* acts as a collection agency for itself, for the federal government and for the municipalities. The municipalities have other local income as well, including ground rents, and have to meet their own expenditure budgets. There is no grant-reduced cost subsidy to homeowners and therefore to residential values as in Britain, but Germany has a system of mortgage interest tax deductions up to a lifetime maximum of 300,000 Deutschemarks (about £120,000) and France limits this form of tax relief to ten years. To the West German a thriving industrial base with low inflation and unemployment is the way to prosperity. The bankers typically own up to 30% of a manufacturing company, which means they use their lending capacity to support industry as a priority, rather than lending to the domestic property markets, which is left to local savings banks. No wonder the Deutschemark has risen in value against sterling by nearly five times since 1960.

Table 4: Britain's 1990/91 Budget

Reformatted for the Incidence of Taxation on the Two Primary Factors of Production
£0,000,000,000s

	Basis of Split	'Land'	'Labour'	Total Budget
Income tax	'Actual'	6.0	53.6	59.6
Social security	Actual	–	36.7	36.7
Value added tax	33/67%	11.9	23.8	35.7
Corporation tax	'Actual'	2.0	17.5	19.5
Local rates	80/20%	11.5	2.9	14.4
Petrol duties	33/67	3.7	7.2	10.9
Tobacco,alcohol,betting	50/50	6.2	6.2	11.3
Car tax	Actual	–	1.3	1.3
Vehicle excise duties	Actual	–	3.0	3.0
Capital gains tax	'Actual'	1.0	0.4	1.4
Inheritance tax	'Actual'	1.0	0.3	1.3
Stamp duties	'Actual'	1.5	0.6	2.1
*Community charge	80/20%	6.1	1.5	7.6
		50.9	155.0	205.9
Percentage		24.7%	75.3%	[100%]
Other receipts – unallocated				20.6
				£226.5 Bn

* treated as 'Local Rates'

The fact is that the tax structure of the UK (and US) economy is farcical. The unfunny part is that with industry in continuing decline, it is just a house built with a pack of cards, housing a nation of small-time property speculators, stuck together with loans that are rapidly coming unstuck. One of Britain's more successful economic sectors is shopkeeping, as Napoleon recognised. With the home manufacturing base in continuous decline and the small geographic size of the country, this entrepreneurial ability just sucks imports straight into consumers' over-valued homes.

Insert 3

'Some Things Never Change'

_____

This letter was sent by the author to the *Daily Telegraph* on 15 September, 1980. The editor did not publish it.

Sir,

In your columns last Friday there was an excellent report on Professor Foster's address to The Association of Metropolitan Authorities, in which he pointed out that the burden of rates on industry was now 35 per cent of its gross profit, and consequently harmful to employment. He also pointed out that the level of central government grant to local authorities was now 61 per cent of their expenditure and the local electorate were not therefore as interested in monitoring expenditure as they would no doubt be if called upon to pay a higher proportion themselves.

What was not mentioned is that the largest single item of expense in the entire national budget is the cost of current grants to Local Authorities, estimated at £14,271 million for 1980-81. This compares with the cost of defence, say at £10,668 million, and government investment in nationalised industries, about which we hear so much, at £648 million.

The cost of these current grants are raised by yet other taxes that are levied principally on the employment, profits and sales of industry and commerce, all of which taxes are by their very nature a disincentive to

---

industrial activity. For example, income tax is actually paid over and borne by the employer, and raises the cost of employing someone very considerably.

The important question is how to raise taxes to cover Local Authority expenditure without harming employment, investment and sales. Professor Foster advocates a local income tax, which on the face of it would not appear to answer this question. However, if there was a general reduction of all taxes on industry, which is the stated aim of this government, and which was financed by a reduction in grants to local authorities, then local rates would have to be raised. This shift in the incidence of taxation would not act as a disincentive to employment, investment in new machinery or to the customer's willingness to buy, and would be a positive factor in making ratepayers more interested in the cost-effectiveness and quality of service provided.

Yours faithfully, S.R.H.

Footnote: Professor Foster, a visiting professor at the London School of Economics and a director of Coopers & Lybrand Associates, management consultants, said that the old rates that 'the non-domestic ratepayers [i.e. industry] pay vastly exceeded the value of the services received – the reverse of the case with the domestic ratepayers. They are a heavy burden on industry and must contribute to the loss of jobs'. By 1991-92, the estimated cost of central government grants had risen to £52.5 billion (1980/81 – £14.3 billion), representing 82% (1980/81 – 61%) of local authority expenditure. The householder contributed 12% in 1990-91 of the cost of local services compared with 10% in 1980-81 and 30% before WW2.

8

The Necessity for Common Markets

Imagine a cartoon of a horizontal human frame, like Swift's Gulliver. This supine form of enforced passivity, however, is John Bull's industrial body. It looks rather old and emaciated, definitely in decline. There is a villain in black standing with a boot on industry's windpipe, who is a tax inspector demanding that the payroll taxes are paid 'by the nineteenth' of the month. A ruffian who has seen better days is pulling on another tender part of the anatomy, who is a trade union demagogue. A landlord measures out the space the body is taking up, together with those attending the scene, including the landlord's own lawyers. But at the feet of this body in decline there is a smartly dressed bureaucrat with a large briefcase, foreign-looking, possibly Belgian, who is tying the ankles together with scarcely visible cords. This person is a protectionist, who does not want foreign competition at home, so the protectionist ties down foreign competitors to keep them out of the market. The workers back home vote for this display of loyalty and shower thanks on the protectionist for saving their 'jobs'.

The most obvious of the scarcely visible cords is trade tariffs, or custom fees payable on imported goods. Less visible cords are quotas on the volume of imports, outright bans and 'voluntary' restraints, often negotiated under threat of retaliation. More invisible still are subsidies given by the home market, both for current expenditure and fixed investment. Even craftier protectionists devise rules and regulations to block imports on technical, safety and quality grounds. If these fail, price fixing on allegations of dumping by foreign manufacturers can be resorted to. Then the home government can alter taxation rates payable by industries, or even let the currency sink on foreign exchange markets to reduce real prices for foreign buyers, or favour domestic suppliers in public procurement. Finally, even more invisible, are the checks on the flow of capital investment across borders, by restriction on foreign ownership and suppression of company and market data.

Britain has always eyed the big and unified American domestic market with a tinge of relish. Not for nothing is it the biggest foreign investor in Uncle Sam by far, with over US$80 billion invested. Growth in world trade is dependent on free trade, and the beggar-my-neighbour approach of protectionism actually reduces world trade by eliminating foreign competition, which ultimately leads to inefficiency, subsidised jobs and higher prices and taxes which are paid for by the home consumer. Realising this, Britain voted in a national referendum in 1975 to ratify its membership in 1973 of the European Economic Community (EEC), which had been established by the Treaty of Rome in 1957. The British voted heavily in favour of free trade. Their American cousins, who are also free traders at heart, were pleased to see their old friends inside the EEC, as their presence would add weight to the anti-protectionist view. For the issue was not just one of free trade inside Europe and inside America, but also one of free trade across the Atlantic between these two great trading blocks, and indeed across the world. Otherwise growth in world trade and therefore in investment, jobs, efficiency and cheaper prices for consumers would be threatened if the EEC developed a 'Fortress Europe' mentality and protected its own industries against foreign imports and competition. The greatest threat to world trade would be if the three major trading blocks, the EEC, the new North American Free Trade Area (formed in 1992, comprising America, Canada and Mexico), and Japan and the 'tiger' economies of the Far East, each went protectionist. It would halt world growth and have the capacity to cause a worldwide depression on its own. The major factor in the Great Depression of the 1930s was America's enactment of the Fordney-McCumber Tariffs in the 1920s even more than the infamous Smoot-Hawley protectionist laws of the 1930s. These enactments led to retaliatory trade barriers being set up by Europe, with a crippling effect on industry in both continents.

It was in recognition of this opportunity and threat that the world community established the General Agreement on Tariffs and Trade (GATT) after WW2. In seven rounds of talks since 1946, GATT has removed tariffs, the most obvious restriction on world trade, on manufactured goods from 40% to 5%. Tariffs, however, are only one form of protectionism. The current Uruguay Round of GATT talks is aimed at liberalising trade in agriculture, textiles and financial services. America alleges that Europe subsidises agriculture with US$12 billion per annum in export subsidies, plus US$25 billion in internal subsidies, whereas America claims to spend only US$1 billion and US$8 billion, respectively. These agricultural subsidies, which are payable under the European Community's Common Agricultural Policy (CAP), are paid to fourteen million farmers, but mainly to smallholder farmers in France and Germany. These CAP subsidies account for 60% of the European Community's budget. British farmers, who are recognised to be very much more efficient and economically viable, receive little benefit from the CAP.

8. The Necessity for Common Markets

The corrupt European argument, promoted mainly by the French, is that there are more farmers per head of population to subsidise. This is hardly surprising, and indicates that the CAP has probably subsidised too many farmers for too long.

Nevertheless in July 1991 the protectionist French foreign trade minister warned that France would never surrender its CAP advantages in the Uruguay Round of GATT talks. The Americans are therefore claiming that taxpayers on both sides of the Atlantic would save US$46 billion per annum if farmers were returned to the free market, and consumers would pay less for their food. This reduction is estimated at £830 less per annum for the average British family. Meanwhile, just consider the effects of this additional taxation on industry, the effect that these subsidies must have on agricultural land values in France and Germany and the effect on inflation caused by these enormous and unnatural distortions in the world economy. France and Germany counter that it is a social and not an economic issue! (They would, wouldn't they?)

In the latest GATT talks at Geneva in 1991, the Americans argued that the CAP budget should be reduced by 75%, but they met a wall of implacable resistance. The dialogue moved to a 30% reduction across the board; then to a 20% reduction in internal price supports, a 36% reduction in export subsidies and a 24% reduction in subsidised tonnage. The talks continue along with the market distortions. It is a frustrating spectacle to observe Creative Persons bargain through the night and day to remove, or Degenerate Persons to maintain, protectionist trade barriers that harm their countries' own consumers and taxpayers and world trade as well. The power of French farmers was amply demonstrated in July 1992 by their blockade of the country's motorway system, which affected much of Continental Europe. More cynically, it has been highlighted too by wanton and inhuman acts of criminality through arson of live animals imported from abroad. The French and German farmer, like any protected sacred cow, is a powerful lobby of Degenerate Persons that puts its own interests firmly first through self-indulgence and myopia. The French and German politicians go along with the anomaly, as there are too many votes at stake.

When Britain voted in 1975 for entry into the EEC the public knew something of what they were voting for as a theoretical model, but not what was in store in practice. On 31 December 1992, the common market as envisaged under the Treaty of Rome will become an actuality in the context of tariff barriers, when this most visible protectionist tool will be systematically reduced throughout the twelve nations of the EC and with other nations belonging to EFTA, such as Switzerland, Sweden and Norway. This is a great step forward and in the right direction towards free trade but surely that is a misprint – 'EC'. No. An 'E' for 'Economic' dropped off the juggernaut rather conveniently on to an autobahn, somewhere in the dark. In 1973 the issue was the establishment of an 'European Economic Community', implying simply a common market, but now the concept is of an 'European Community', a quite different proposition. When the bureaucrats got down to the details, they soon discovered that it was impossible to create a truly common market by the removal of trade tariffs alone, as there were also the other less visible barriers, namely the subsidies, particularly the vast agricultural subsidies under the CAP, quotas, quality regulations, capital restrictions, foreign exchange and taxation variables mentioned above. There would have to be a Federal Euro-Government, as in America. Although nations, like leopards, do not change their spots, the Eurocrats now had their hearts and minds focused on a central super-state government, arguably nearer the spirit of Moscow than Washington.

Their first problem was that the EC has twelve different currencies, so the European Currency Unit (ECU) was created. So far so good, but that could not stop the Italians or British or anyone else fiddling the actual rate of exchange of the lira or pound in any number of ways, and thereby tilting the playing field down-hill in their favour by reducing the price of their exports to other members. So there would have to be European Monetary Union (EMU) to keep the common market level by the introduction of a single currency. Then the debate moved to the necessity to create a European Central Bank (ECB), which will probably have to be run by the Germans as they have the strongest currency, to set interest rates for the ECU. Before that enormous step could be taken, there was still the need to sustain a fair common market by some form of agreed exchange rates between individual currencies, and so a fixed Exchanged Rate Mechanism (ERM) was created in the meantime as an opportunity for currency convergence. The Deutschemark effectively governs the ERM, as it is the strongest currency. Unfortunately Chancellor Kohl overrode President Poehl of the Bundesbank and in 1990 fixed the weak East German Ostmark at parity with the strong West German Deutschemark for the first 4,000 Ostmarks per saver and at two-to-one thereafter. A more realistic rate would have been something like seventeen-to-one. The result only increased the unquantified cost of an already expensive reunification with East Germany and has forced up German interest rates. Therefore interest rates throughout Europe, because of the fixed exchange rate system imposed by the ERM, have also risen at exactly the wrong point in the business cycle during the 1991-92 worldwide recession. The pathetic sight of Britain's Chancellor of the Exchequer pleading with the German Bundes-bank to hold interest rates down only goes to show how the ERM now, and EMU in the future, will hand economic management of each member's economy to the centre, which is exactly what the federalist Eurocrats want to happen anyway.

The system of fixed rates proved untenable for the weaker currencies and on 16 September 1992 Britain and Italy left the ERM and Spain devalued by 5% within it. The real causes of this realignment were that Britain had joined at too high a rate in 1990 and that Germany was entering the world recession two years after Britain. The delay was caused by the Ostmark's replacement by the Deutschemark, which boosted West German demand from the East, as well as inflation and monetary expansion, thus requiring German interest rates to rise just as Britain's were already falling. It was a classic example of a man-induced distortion to the short-term cycle, of Ecu-nomics over eco-nomics, creating a problem of timing and convergence for EMU. The problem will not go away for members within the ERM, as Germany's current account deficit soars in 1993 through recession and reunification creating a funding gap estimated at 150 billion Deutschemarks and rising. When the German electorate realises the situation, when interest and tax rates rise and recession intensifies, Bonn will come under public pressure, and opposition to EMU and even reunification could also intensify in 1994-95. The next flaw in Chancellor Kohl's reunification deal will then bite, as he promised pay parity to East Germans by 1995. They are a fifth of the population but only produce 7% of Pan-German GDP. More 'work creation' schemes will no doubt corrupt more data.

In December 1991 the EC members signed the Treaty of Maastricht, a sub-treaty of the Treaty of Rome, setting out the road towards EMU. British hesitation was translated into an opt-out clause and the date for Britain to join EMU was put back formally to 1 January 1998, although final decisions will be taken before 31 December 1996. If Britain notifies its intention to move to full EMU status, it will give up its 'powers in the field of monetary policy according to national law', says the protocol. The Bank of England will become a 'national central bank' and will subscribe its share of capital to the new ECB and will 'transfer to the ECB foreign reserve assets' on the same basis as other members. In return Britain will then have the right to participate in the appointment of the President, Vice-President and other members of the Executive Board of the ECB. Britain will be well and truly federalised at that point, with its interest and exchange rates and aspects of fiscal legislation run from the centre. The minimum rate for VAT in the EC has, for example, already been agreed. Prime Minister Major countered with his own idea of a 'Hard ECU' that would act as the anchor for the ERM. Each member's own currency would be worth so many Hard ECUs and be fixed by normal market operations. The beauty in theory for the British is that they would not necessarily hand over sovereignty of sterling, and therefore of interest and exchange rates, to be managed at the centre. The problem for the federalist Eurocrat is that the wily Brits could still alter their exchange rates by running down sterling and asking for settlement in good old pounds.

In May 1992 the Danish electorate voted out the Treaty of Maastricht. On September 20th the French, who were the original architects of EMU, underwhelmingly endorsed the Treaty of Maastricht, which requires the unanimous approval of all EC member states, by a margin of less than 1%. The fact still is that the Deutschemark remains a currency whirlpool at the centre of the EC, whether sterling is in the ERM or not. Prime Minister Major's opt-out clause, so painstakingly negotiated at Maastricht, always did look redundant. The fate of Maastricht, which still fails to be endorsed by Denmark, does not alter the fundamental terms of the Treaty of Rome. Europe and Britain have no option but to move towards a common market, which still takes a significant step on 31 December 1992, when the remaining tariffs are meant to be removed progressively.

Nevertheless there is more than enough diplomatic negotiation and actual implementation of basic free-market requirements to be worked on, as is amply demonstrated by the GATT negotiations on the agricultural subsidies of the CAP. In fact CAP is but one specific area, for there are similar distortions in manufacturing and capital markets which thwart the existence of a true free trade zone. For example, the European electronics industry will receive 5.7 billion ECUs from the EC between 1990 and 1994, with additional funding from individual members. (An ECU is worth about 77.5 pence.) In addition, European semi-conductor manufacturers wish to maintain the present 40% tariff rate on imports, particularly Philips in Holland and Groupe Bull in France. IBM owns a 5.7% stake worth US$100 million in Groupe Bull, in addition to its stake in Intel Corporation, the leading American manufacturer of these devices, and has also formed an alliance with Siemens AG to produce the world's most advanced memory chips. The tariff is aimed against Japanese manufacturers like NEC, but IBM which is formally and actually American, is also really European and nearly Japanese too, in view of that firm's historical commitment to Europe and its growing interests in Japan. Firms like IBM and NEC are truly international and competitive. IBM, for example, assembles 'American' computers in Japan for export to the EC.

8. The Necessity for Common Markets

Raising tariffs against these efficient multinationals in order to protect lesser players is not a winning strategy for anyone in the long term. While those firms the tariffs were designed to protect are unlikely to be saved by such mollycoddling, the taxpayer and consumer suffer higher taxes and higher prices, which naturally benefit landowners, as they reflect immediately into higher land values. The fact is that, in the meantime, IBM and NEC are Europe's leading suppliers of computers and semi-conductors anyway.

Trade within the EC is distorted by massive subsidies in such areas as agriculture, coal mining, atomic power, railways and general manufacturing. The European Commission is investigating subsidies to Groupe Bull of France (6 billion French Francs), the Italian truck industry (287 billion lire), Belgium's Sabena airlines (35 billion Belgian Francs) and a dozen others, including Renault and British Aerospace's supremely illogical, unnecessary and ill-timed acquisition of Rover Cars, involving £48 million of taxpayers' 'sweeteners'. (Rover's future could never possibly have been with an aircraft manufacturer. Honda of Japan already owns 20% of Rover, and Rover is 'Honda' spelt backwards as regards its strategic future.) The Germans do not feature strongly in the subsidy hit-list, but that is only because the European Commission has not got round to investigating subsidised loans to industries, provided by shareholding bankers and organisations like KFW (Credit Institute for Reconstruction). And all this is before we consider the issue that concerns British industry most, namely the openness of capital markets. British companies quoted on the stock exchange can be bid for from abroad, subject only to monopoly considerations. No other European capital markets reflect this openness, for the non-availability of public information on the continent is only matched by entrenched shareholder attitudes and practices. For example, in Germany only 2,000 public companies are required to disclose information to a level approaching requirements affecting many thousands of British companies, many of them privately owned.

Within the EC, British target companies accounted for 73% of the total of foreign takeovers in the whole EC in 1988. There are major differences in shareholder rights, such as voting rights and bearer shares which are of uncertain ownership and not easily traceable. There are major accounting differences as well. For example, the largest German insurer, Allianz, carries investments in its books at original cost – meaning if it invested in a company at one Deutschemark in 1970, or 1920, then it writes off any higher price it subsequently pays. Quite simply, the true extent of its hidden reserves are massive but unknown. Therefore there is the need to make companies takeover-proof, by cross-shareholdings and other obstructions, as their stock market values are probably massively understated and dividend pay-outs are much below the British norm. In effect the levels of dividends in Germany are a type of subsidy, in that companies retain more cash and therefore borrow less, but this can suit the banks as they are also shareholders and their deposits are consequently higher. In Germany the banks tell industry what their budgets for next year are going to be, including how much cash should end up in the bank.

The EC has much basic ground to clear to achieve even a free trade area. The attempts to rush towards the federal-type issues like monetary union to achieve a truly common market smacks of politically-inspired, strategic ambushes to move control to the centre, without the centre having to remove its strategic defences, such as the CAP and Ostmark/Deutschemark and German pay parity, at the same speed. It seems improbable that an ERM strategy can work while the leader of the pack is bogged down anyway with the integration of 20% of its enlarged population, namely the 17,000,000 inhabitants of the former East Germany. Industrial production in the east is down in 1992 by an unbelievable 66% and unemployment is approaching 3,000,000, while pay levels are five times higher than in neighbouring Czechoslovakia. They are economically and ecologically bankrupt, and the German tactic of raising interest rates and running a current account deficit, rather than raising their own domestic tax rates, will be seen for what it is: an export of insolvency, courtesy of the ERM, to other members of the EC. For Britain the risk of joining the ERM at the mid-rate of 2.95 Deutschemarks in October 1990 was an otherwise unnecessary lengthening of the recession. To have continued in the ERM in the current band would have produced an even longer recession. This did not happen as the foreign exchange markets swamped the politicians and forced realignment. Detachment from the ERM will free Britain from Germany's reunification mistakes and from the other problems on her borders, particularly to the East. Germany's ability to make mistakes was recently confirmed by its immediate diplomatic recognition of Croatia, against international advice, that did nothing to prevent the outbreak of civil war in former Yugoslavia. Britain cannot handle Germany's problems, but can at least now manage its own economy. That little stretch of water called the English Channel will enable Britain to keep a clearer perspective on how the EC should evolve its unity. This is Britain's historic role in the affairs of the European continent, and one she has played well in the maintenance of freedom and democracy. Germany, however, intends to create a 'two-speed' Europe. This phraseology smacks of *Vorsprung Durch*

Technik and sounds important, but the truth is that EMU is the cloak over the Franco-German love-in, courtesy of the CAP.

There is no especial reason why Britain should aim for EMU. Switzerland has no interest in doing so. Nor has Sweden. Britain and Italy both left the ERM on Whirlwind Wednesday, 16 September 1992. In Italy the private sector has the highest savings ratio in the world and it evades taxation, while the state is over-borrowed and there is no political stability. The opposite is true of Britain. An OECD forecast published in July 1992 showed Italy's government debt at 112.1% of GDP, while Britain's was only 41.7%, the lowest of any G7 member. (The US's was 60.8%, Japan's 58.8% and Germany's 44.8%.) So, when interest rates rise, the Italians are not bothered as they earn more on their savings while the state disintegrates, but the British suffer with their higher personal debts, mostly related to property, while their government tells them that the pain is good for them. The Germans have a chance to luxuriate in *Schadenfreude* as they watch the British squirm in their houses and Italian state industries go broke, with every upward twist of interest rates caused by reunification. You cannot blame the Germans just for being in a position to witness what is happening to others, but Kohl can be blamed for rushing towards EMU with the various economies having such diverse structures. Forcing the members into the same monetary mould promises to break a lot of old bones.

For Europe to replicate federal America will take several decades. Even then the Germans will be seeking to control the centre, the French will be being French, the British will be seeking to manage the balance of power from the touchline, the Greeks will be bringing gifts and asking for subsidies, and exclusivity for an Italian will still be the first seventeen customers through the door, whatever the EC regulations. The practical economist must allow for the nature of people and of nations, and for their Creative and Degenerate characteristics. Unity in diversity should be accepted as the rule and creating a basic free trade area within and without the first objective, with the accent on democracy not on bureaucracy. In terms of external reciprocity, the Institute for International Economics calculates that America still protects, through visible trade barriers, between 16% and 18% of its imports in 1991, while Japan protects about 25% of its imports by tariffs but is also a leading exponent of less visible barriers based on quality and technical constraints. Japan however, is moving in the direction of freeing up her own market. As her economy and worldwide interests integrate into the global economy as a major force, her best interests are served by a free trade policy as well. To work towards free trade is the right strategic thrust for Britain and for Europe and the detail of federal-wide issues, such as taxation and exchange rates, must be allowed plenty of time to evolve. Britain's slogan should be 'GATT not CAP'. For the tenth fundamental principle of economics is that the right balance between land and labour can only reach optimum fruition in conditions of free trade. This is a necessary precondition for a so-called exporting and manufacturing country like Britain, which still has a long way to go to reorganise its own economic structure to achieve an effective working fiscal balance between property and industry. Until that is achieved British membership of the ERM is not a practical priority in the short term. While German discipline and determination will undoubtedly succeed in reunification in the long term, the 1990s promise to be a roller-coaster for the enlarged German economy in terms of interest and tax rates. The possibility of Old King Kohl failing to take one of the sharper bends on the high-speed Franco-German vision of an united Europe, tipping a post-referendum Mitterand out in the process at the GATT/CAP chicane turn, should not be underestimated. At least half of their respective countrymen would laugh at the sight, clap their hands and say that the delicate ERM should never have been allowed out on roads with that many bumps and pot-holes in the first place.

Insert 4

'It's All a Question of Timing'

This letter from the author was published in *The Times* on 16 July 1992. The editor deleted the second and last paragraphs.

Sir,

Mr Lamont [The Chancellor of the Exchequer] states that he intends to maintain sterling in the ERM and move to the narrower band in order to reduce inflation to below 2%, regardless of the depth and effects of the continuing recession.

The Chancellor should heed a cautionary tale of the Sufi mystic, the Mulla Nasrudin, called 'All I needed was time'. The Mulla bought a donkey and decided to economise by giving it less food every day. When the donkey was reduced to almost no food at all, it fell over and died. 'Pity,' thought the Mulla. 'If I had had a little more time before it died, I could have got it accustomed to living on nothing at all.'

The Chancellor's aim of reducing inflation will at some point coincide with the lowest level of economic activity since WW2. The Chancellor is addressing the wrong problems at the wrong point in the economic cycle. The problem is in the mismanagement of the upswing, for example in the badly timed expansionary budgets of 1974 and 1988. The time to have joined the ERM was in 1985, not in 1990, in order to restrain the boom. The Chancellor would then have been in a position to reflate gently in 1992/93, but harness the next recovery with timely interest rate and prudent fiscal management.

The donkey must have been hurting, but it definitely stopped working. Time will tell whether the Chancellor will share the same fate or whether he will stay alive, but as sorrowful as the Mulla when he surveys the result of his restrictive regime. It's all a question of timing.

Yours faithfully, S.R.H.

Footnote: Mr Lawson, who was a predecessor of Mr Lamont, wanted to join the ERM in 1985, but Mrs Thatcher blocked him. Mr John Major, who was Mr Lamont's immediate predecessor, persuaded Mrs Thatcher to join the ERM in October 1990, when the recession was an actuality for everyone other than the Treasury. Mr Major, as Prime Minister, said in 1991 that 'if the recession isn't hurting, it isn't working'. The ERM was hurting sterling and on 16th September 1992 it stopped working. Mr Lamont wore a smile from ear to ear. His wife said she had heard him singing in the bath for the first time! He was as happy for the prospect of economic recovery as the Mulla would have been if his donkey had come back to life.

9

An Economic Portrait of the 1980s

Britain and America are as close as two countries ever will be in strategic objectives, whether cultural, economic or military. 'Two great countries divided by a common language!' was how Sir Winston Churchill put it (and he was an Anglo-American). The relationship looks set to continue, as the relationship does with the Commonwealth, regardless of Britain's place in the EC. The development of the British and American economies since WW2 has been remarkably similar given their vastly different size, and this was never so evident as in the 1980s. The British economy reflects new trends in the American economy, albeit after a brief time-lag and with modifications. Moreover, nearly two-fifths of the earnings of companies quoted on the International Stock Exchange, London are derived in US dollars from American operations. Quite simply, if America goes up, Britain goes up and vice versa. Whether Britain is a member of the EC or not, what happens in the American economy is strategically influential to Britain. The purpose of sketching a portrait of the two economies in the 1980s is to set out the extraordinary successes and failures of this decade. It will also highlight the grievous mistakes on both sides of the Atlantic in managing, or not managing, the balance between land and labour.

The decade of the 1980s was almost certainly the fifth short cycle on the back of the upswing of the long cycle. (God forbid that it was the first short cycle of the long downswing, but time will tell!) It saw two remarkably similar leaders with very similar economic beliefs and convictions. Margaret Thatcher, a grocer's daughter from Lincolnshire, became Prime Minister and First Lord of the Treasury in June 1979. She stayed on for a record consecutive eleven years until her own party ditched her in November 1990. Ronald Reagan, a former B-movie actor from Iowa, was President of America from November 1980 until November 1988. Both their periods of office began in a severe recession. Both administrations achieved spectacular economic recovery. Both then made terrible economic errors. And they both left economies crippled with horrendous debt in the private sector. America's Federal debt was also especially crippling. It stood at US$909 billion in 1980, but by 1988 had nearly tripled to US$2.6 trillion. By the end of 1992, it will have risen to over US$4 trillion, equivalent to US$28,800 per worker compared with US$8,495 per worker in 1980. Under Thatcher, on the other hand, Britain was actually a net repayer of national debt for a short time during the three years 1988-90, although by 1992 the current account external deficit was once again rising towards £12 billion and the PSBR requirement to cover the domestic budgetary deficit was rising to £13.8 billion in 1991-92, on to £28.1 billion in 1992-93 and heading for over £40 billion in 1993-94.

The transatlantic recession which got underway towards the end of 1979 peaked in 1981. Shortly after President Reagan was elected, the US prime rate hit 21.5%, its highest level ever, and Britain's base rate rose to 17%. Both economies were suffering from runaway inflation. When Thatcher took office, inflation was already soaring through 10% per annum and heading for over 20% in 1980. The late 1970s had seen the advance of the monetarist theories of Professor Milton Friedman of Chicago. He coined the phrase that 'there is no such thing as a free lunch' to underline his basic tenet that monetary growth was the root cause of inflation. In simple terms, the more the money in circulation, the higher the prices go and the more the lunch will inevitably cost. Both Thatcher and Reagan determined to counter inflation by adopting the monetarists' favoured approach of raising interest rates, encouraging productivity by tax cuts and curbing the monopolistic power of the trade unions. During the 1960s and 1970s, the power of organised trade unions had grown unchecked and the belief had also grown that increases in wages were the prime force driving the inflationary spiral. Reagan wasted no time in tackling the unions in 1981. At great political risk he sacked the nation's entire force of over thirty thousand air traffic controllers, whose strike was paralysing the nation's key coast-to-coast transportation system and the economy. It was a bold move and it worked, as controllers drifted back to work and signed new contracts.

Thatcher's government introduced new legislation to curb trade union power by outlawing the 'closed shop' regime, under which workers in many of Britain's factories had no free vote on key issues like strike action. This introduction of democracy on to the factory floor was a major achievement. Days lost through 'wildcat' strikes, when no ballot amongst workers to vote on the unions' strike call was allowed, disappeared almost overnight. Thatcher's real fight with the unions came in 1984-85, when Arthur Scargill once again led the miners on a year-long, politically inspired strike. The strike was violent and one miner in South Wales was murdered as he went to work in a taxi. Degenerate Persons dropped a concrete slab from a bridge over a motorway onto the vehicle. It was perhaps a fitting symbol for the death of union power too, which had seen the autocratic misuse of their position by many union leaders ever since Hugh Scanlon led the Coventry toolroom dispute after WW2, which was the start of A^{2}LOB^2 and corruption of time standards. In 1982, however, Thatcher stood firm and saw Scargill off. The National Union of Mineworkers was split, as the Nottingham miners set up their own independent Union of Democratic Mineworkers in 1984. Thatcher and Reagan broke the union monopoly of labour, but neither touched the other great monopoly, that of the landowner.

One of the real seeds of financial destruction for the 1980s was sown by President Carter earlier that same year when he signed in March the Depository Institutions Deregulation and Monetary Control Act. Carter was a (former) peanut farmer who had not the slightest idea what he was signing for. This legislation inspired deregulation of money markets on both sides of the Atlantic. American banks could now pay interest on checking and saving accounts. Savings & Loan institutions (S&Ls), equivalent to Britain's ubiquitous building societies, could now pay market interest rates on deposits. For the first time S&Ls were therefore forced to offer higher rates on deposits than they traditionally earned on mortgages. The same legislation also raised Federal insurance on S&L deposit accounts from US\$40,000 to US\$100,000, thereby swelling the S&L deposit base. The S&Ls were forced to pursue high-risk business which they did not understand and which was often fraudulent. Mrs Thatcher also determined to break the bankers' monopoly by deregulating the financial services industry in Britain as well. In 1983 she followed suit and authorised building societies to broaden the scope of their lending away from their traditional business of providing mortgages to home owners. In effect, they were free to become banks, and banks did their best to enter the home mortgages' market in a competitive free-for-all. Unwittingly Thatcher and Carter had unleashed the credit boom that would drive the spectacular growth of the 1980s but end in bust in the early 1990s. Thatcher had also previously removed all foreign exchange controls in 1979, as she was convinced that market forces should drive exchange rates.

Both Reagan and Thatcher were determined to reduce income taxes in order to put more money in consumers' pockets, so that consumer demand would lead their economies out of recession. Thatcher reduced the higher rate of income tax from 83% to 60% as a first step, a dramatic reduction which in itself inspired a confidence based on relief. She also abolished the investment income surcharge of 15%, which meant that the top rate of tax on all income was effectively cut from 98% to 60%. Reagan also cut income tax by 5% in October 1981, by a further 10% in July 1982 and by a further 10% in July 1983. He also granted tax incentives for the construction of office buildings and apartments, just as Thatcher had done in the previous year with the creation of 'enterprize zones' in derelict urban areas, where private investors could deduct the cost of their investment from their taxable income. These fiscal measures, together with the steady reduction in interest rates from 1980 onwards, fuelled economic recovery but also provided conditions which led to a boom in property values and feverish construction of buildings of all types on both sides of the Atlantic. It is significant that the seeds of the 1991-92 recession were sown in both economies as early as 1981. In October 1981 Reagan also signed a Bill raising the level of Federal debt above US$1 trillion for the first time, which he announced was 'a monument to the policies of the past, policies which as of today are reversed'. Reagan's optimism and forecasting ability, however, would have made him a prime candidate as a Mandarin at the UK Treasury.

In 1982 interest rates declined further and economic activity picked up, although unemployment, which in America reached nearly 11%, failed to respond quickly. Already in early 1982 the National Savings and Loan League asked Congress for US$15.5 billion to insure deposits of ailing S&Ls. The problems brought on by Carter's crazy 1980 legislation were surprisingly quick to appear. Nevertheless the reduction in interest rates and economic recovery fed indirectly into the housing market in both America and Britain and prices started rising strongly. The surge in house prices sucked in frantic buyers, who saw prices climbing out of their reach and who then became desperate to get on the home-owning bandwagon. Borrowers assumed that inflation would reduce the real value of their debts or that interest rates would never go up, but that house prices would continue to rise. During the 1980s, house prices in both economies in real terms rose by up to two-and-a-half times. In March 1983 OPEC cut the price of oil from US$34 to US$29 a barrel. This had a beneficial effect on inflation and enabled both governments to hold interest rates down, thereby contributing to the credit boom and directly causing land values to rise still further.

The merger boom was also getting into its stride, and in 1984 Standard Oil merged with Gulf Corporation in a US$13.3 billion deal, which dwarfed Du Pont's US$7.5 billion acquisition of Conoco in August 1981. Big was good on Wall Street, and what was good for Wall Street was good for the City of London too. As the merger boom got going, Michael Milken, a fixed-interest dealer in Drexel Burnham Lambert's West Coast operation, began to peddle his high-yielding 'junk bonds' to the S&L and insurance industries, which now required these higher yields in the newly deregulated marketplace. The management buy-out (MBO) syndrome was spawned and the era of the highly leveraged transaction (HLT) put the merger/MBO market into top gear. These new financial structures soon found their way across the Atlantic and became a major feature of the deal-driven 1980s. The MBO movement was originally intended by Creative Persons to enable existing managers to acquire the businesses they ran from their larger corporate owners, thereby replacing corporate shackles with management freedom and incentives. For example, the highly successful MBO of National Freight Corporation by Barclays Merchant Bank transformed the efficiency of the whole operation, as highly motivated managers and employees realised the opportunity to add value to their shares. The HLT features, however, were soon adopted by Degenerate Persons to enable corporate raiders to go on a hostile takeover binge. HLTs were financed on wafer-thin permanent capital. This higher leverage or gearing (i.e. high level of borrowings in relation to permanent capital) at times reached 1,000% or more of the permanent capital, as opposed to the more normal 50% to 100% level. The theory was that disposals of non-strategic operations would be made quickly by the new unit to reduce the weight of the borrowings, but as the decade wore on the deal merchants forgot their own rules. When a major retailer which had been financed by junk bonds inevitably went bust, Michael Milken confessed that his team had never factored into their sums the possibility that sales might at some point decrease! As soon as sales inevitably turned down in the short cycle, this and many other leveraged transactions were bankrupt. Many viewed Milken as a financial wizard, but he was clearly unaware of even the existence of business cycles, which is the first lesson for any financier, let alone their practical implications.

Nowhere was this breathless rush for profit more evident than in the run-up to October 1986 for the City of London's 'Big Bang'. This explosive metaphor was chosen to name the day when the stock exchange became an electronic market as opposed to a floor-based market where brokers looked into each other's eyes and where their 'word was their bond'. (New York had first moved to screen-based trading in 1973.) Practically every bank in Britain and many American and European banks scrambled to get a seat at the table for the forthcoming feast of global securities trading, where London was in a convenient time-zone slot linking Tokyo and Hong Kong with New York, Chicago and Los Angeles. Partners in venerable firms of stockbrokers, who had been used to earning a good salary and bonus in a bull market and then eking out a relative pittance in the ensuing bear market, sat back and listened. The competing buyers offered them vast sums for goodwill, guaranteed salary and bonus packages and other perks in all seasons, come rain or shine. The eminent house of Cazenove & Co decided to remain independent and procured a large line of credit for underwriting from Bank of Scotland, which had wisely decided to keep out of this volatile business. Every other major broking house was sold.

The new integrated securities houses recruited 'yuppies' and 'dinkies' who had to drive around in Porsches and BMWs, while champagne and wine bars mushroomed on every corner, creating a mirage of property values. The older partners could not believe their luck, and as soon as their 'golden handcuffs' were off, having served their new masters for the minimum contractual periods they retired to the country as happy BOBOs – 'Burnt Out But Opulent'. In the meantime those archetypal Degenerate Persons, estate agents, saw what the stockbrokers were doing and decided there was no reason why they should not invent their own bandwagon and capitalise on the raging property markets. The personal financial services market was fuelled by the property boom. The big insurance companies and some banks purchased over-valued chains of estate agents, even paying around £50,000 for a small branch in a market town. The theory was that as people bought a house and arranged a mortgage to pay for it, they could be sold pension plans, insurance and life assurance at the same time. This was not an incorrect theory, at least in a rising market. Much of the vast consideration paid for these partnership-type businesses found its way back into the property market, as the happy owners who had sold out now traded up-market and bought new homes. It all looked so sensible in 1986, but by 1990 most of the purchasers had lost their money. The natural cycles go on.

The general public are entitled to ask if anyone in authority realised what was going on. More important, did anyone issue a warning on where this merry-go-round would lead? In fact, as early as 7 June 1984 the Chairman of the Securities and Exchange Commission, John Shad, had warned in the clearest terms that the 'more leveraged takeovers and buy-outs today, the more bankruptcies tomorrow'. These prophetic words fell on the deaf ears of the raging bull market driven by Degenerate Persons, and the MBO and HLT booms went on regardless. In 1985 the Chairman of the Federal Reserve, Paul Volcker, warned in February that corporate debt was growing too quickly on account of the 'huge volume of mergers, leveraged buy-outs and stock repurchases'. Paul Volcker and his successor, Alan Greenspan, repeatedly voiced their concern. That did not deter Macy's, the New York department store, from being privatised later in 1985 in a US$3.6 billion management buy-out. This deal collapsed into bankruptcy in early 1992, following hard on the trail of Bloomingdale's. Surprisingly the US Treasury Department stated on 6 December 1985 that it was 'adamantly opposed', as a Degenerate Person would be, to a Federal Reserve recommendation for curbing hostile takeovers financed by high-yield, high-risk junk bonds. In case there was any doubt that economic naïveté existed in the highest offices of the land, Reagan one week later signed the Gramm-Rudman-Hollings Deficit-Reduction Amendment that was meant to bring the budget into balance within five years, by 1991. (In fact, in 1991 the Federal budget deficit turned out to be US$269 billion.) In May 1987 the Governor of the Bank of England publicly warned bankers about the seriously over-heated property market in Britain, and again in 1989 in Paris. Mrs Thatcher had become alarmed about the level of personal debt and she symbolically returned her own credit cards and warned the banks against mail-shots soliciting borrowers for their expensive plastic-based loans.

In 1986 the price of oil fell from US$25 to US$10 per barrel, and the oil-based Texan economy took a plunge. Texas was the first state where the property bubble collapsed and the local S&Ls started going bust by the day. Before the recession had even taken hold of the economy in the early 1990s, every single bank in Texas defaulted, putting an enormous strain on the already overblown Federal banking system. The year 1986 also saw the first insider dealing scandal spawned by the booming stock market. When a dealer at Drexel Burnham Lambert was arrested, he pointed the finger at a fellow Degenerate, a Russian emigré so-called financier, who bought shares on the New York Stock Exchange just before they soared on takeover announcements, based on inside information. The latter was also arrested and the American authorities tipped off British investigators about dealings ahead of the Irish brewer Guinness's takeover of Scotland's Distillers Company earlier in the year, which was the biggest hostile takeover ever seen in London. This stock market boom was characterised by questionable practice in high places and a distinct lack of probity amongst professional advisers. This particularly unpleasant face of Degenerate Person, however, also manifested itself in the Japanese stock market where some promoters unashamedly favoured politicians while using criminal tendencies to put the squeeze on incumbent shareholders and managers by strong-arm market tactics. The professions of accountancy and law also saw a marked decline in professional standards, which will produce much more comment and analysis as the inevitable DTI investigations, reports and lawsuits unfold.

The boom continued in the early months of 1987. Between January and August the Dow Jones Industrial Average rose by over 40% and the London FT-SE 100 by more than a third, both fuelled by annual growth running at over 40%. Reagan started the year, however, by submitting the first trillion dollar budget. More than six months later the new Chairman of the Federal Reserve, Alan Greenspan, stated: 'It is absolutely essential [that the Federal Reserve's] central focus be on restraining inflation because if that fails, then we have very little opportunity for sustained long-term economic growth.' His clear reasoning meant that he knew he had no option but to put up interest rates to reduce economic activity and bring down inflation. It was clear that as early as July 1987 he saw the inevitability of the ensuing downturn and that he knew he had to cool the economy. There appeared to be no similar perception in Britain, alas, where interest rates were still declining from 10% to 8%. Less than three months later, the Dow Jones Industrial Average plunged 261 points between 14-16 October as thirty-year Treasury Bonds soared two percentage points in four months to 10.2%. These higher interest rates were rapidly followed by 'Black Monday' on 19 October. There was a worldwide stock market meltdown and the Dow and the FT-SE 100 both fell over 500 points on the same day, along with every other stock market. This was an extraordinary worldwide phenomenon. The message sent by the stock markets of the world was that the party really was over. No one wanted to listen and no one wanted to accept the implications. In fact the authorities reacted over the next two years to keep the boom alive and only made things worse, far worse.

This amazing stock market crash contained a fundamental message. The G7 economies, with the exception of West Germany, were over-heated and over-borrowed, and the peak of the 90-year long cycle was approaching. The 45-year upward curve would soon become the 45-year downward curve. In the autumn of 1988 the Berlin Wall came down and then even financially conservative West Germany joined the takeover trial, not by buying companies, but by impulsively taking over the whole of the bankrupt East German Republic with its 17,000,000 poorly fed, poorly housed and poorly skilled population. This ' takeover' was formally acknowledged two years later. This historic move meant that Germany avoided recession as the former East Germans spent their valuable new Deutschemarks buying washing-machines and cars. When this inflationary bonanza had been spent, it was inevitable that Germany would also enter the worldwide recession in late-1992, as the unforeseen and massive bills for reunification came home to roost. German interest rates would rise towards 10% in 1992 and inflation would reach 4% per annum, the highest since 1974.

The extraordinary fact is that government agencies, bankers and business-men continued for nearly three more years after 1987's 'Black Monday' to carry on with the binge. With the British budget of March 1988, the Chancellor of the Exchequer, Nigel Lawson, formulated the most disastrous financial cocktail since WW2, with more damaging consequences than even Lord Barber's ill-conceived budgets of 1972-74 which were crafted with the objective of 5% annual growth! All these budgets sought to expand the economy, by both fiscal and monetary means, as the short 9-year cycles were already cresting. Barber's budgets led to inflation in 1973-76 of 9.7%, 16.5% and 26.1%, as property values surged. Lawson's 1988 budget was hailed by Mrs Thatcher at the time as the most successful budget ever. To be fair to Lawson, his expansionary budget was in part a knee-jerk reaction to the shock to confidence caused by 'Black Monday' the previous autumn, whereas Lord Barber's budget was simply an ill-timed 'dash for growth'. Lawson reduced base rate to 7.5% in May 1988, having reduced the higher rate of income tax from 60% to 40%, unleashing an unstoppable combination of demand-pull credit-push expansion. Lawson subsequently claimed that this interest rate reduction was made at the suggestion of Mrs Thatcher. 'To my eternal regret I accepted the poisoned chalice,' he wrote in 1992. The growth was reflected immediately in surging property values rather than in industrial investment, which requires a much longer lead-time. Lawson's budget contained one specific measure that fed directly into the housing market. Double tax relief on mortgage interest for two persons buying a property together would be available until August. The live-in lovers, lesbians and homosexuals formed an orderly queue with Sloane rangers, sharing yuppies, caring school pals and brothers and sisters outside the mortgage shop, while property speculators rubbed their hands in glee. Together with cheaper credit, the bottom rung of the housing ladder was stoked up and fuelled a further rise for the whole housing market. In 1988 bank lending rose by a quarter in Britain. By early 1989 interest rates were forced back up to 12% as demand for credit soared and the annual increase in M4 lending reached £90 billion. Catastrophe was bound to follow.

The spring of 1988 also saw Donald Trump, the New York financier, announce that he would buy the New York Plaza Hotel for US$410 million and add yet a third casino in Atlantic City in 1989. He also paid over US$300 million for a shuttle airline. All three transactions were financed mainly by bank loans and junk bonds.The perceptions of the Federal Reserve on where the economy was heading had not communicated themselves to the financial markets. The credit-financed boom turned Trump into a billionaire owner who owed over a billion. The inevitable downturn turned Trump into a chump by 1990, which does not say a lot for the bankers who financed him.

Amazingly, the largest bank in both America and Britain each decided to raise more capital and in 1988-90 they both went on a lending binge into the overblown property sector. Citicorp in the US raised US$560 million Preferred Shares, convertible into 15% of the bank's capital, from a Saudi Prince, Al-Waleed bin Talal. Then the bank continued lending merrily on property in the North East corridor of America, when it was clear that the market was already falling. In 1992 Citicorp's non-performing loans are about US$15 billion against shareholders' funds of US$13.5 billion. Barclays Bank in Britain raised £920 million in the London market in late 1988. Most of this new capital funded commercial property. Barclays Bank's 1991 accounts have since confirmed that it has lent £5.4 billion to commercial property companies, which is nearly equal to its entire share capital and reserves of £5.7 billion. In fact, the true figure of all lending on property is far higher as, in common with other banks, the greater proportion of the rest of any bank's lending is in one way or another secured indirectly on assumed property values. In 1991 Barclays also had £11.1 billion of UK residential mortgages and £9.5 billion of personal loans, the greater part of which will be secured on property. In addition loans to agriculture were £1.8 billion. The total UK loan book of £56 billion was 50% secured on property on disclosed data. When other lending to industry secured by way of property is taken into account, the lending secured on property could even amount to over six times the bank's capital and reserves. Barclays commercial property lending was £1 billion in 1988, £1.3 billion in 1989, £800 million in 1990, but only £132 million in 1991 as reality dawned. When such visible institutions carry on lending in this way, their misplaced enthusiasm proves infectious and foreign banks were quick to follow their lead, particularly Japanese banks.

The raging bull market got into bankers' heads in other ways as well. The highly leveraged takeovers required such massive syndication among banks that conflicts of interest issues began to surface. The luckless Barclays carried off the wooden spoon in these stakes as well. Avaricious eyes of Degenerate Persons in the City were cast in the direction of Lord Weinstock's GEC (General Electic Company) which was making around £800 million profit per annum and was sitting on £1.5 billion cash. A £2 company (literally two pounds of share capital) was formed called Metsun, which would launch a hostile, American-style HLT bid for GEC. Barclays agreed to be the lead banker, but it was also a main banker for GEC. The bid was ill-conceived and failed. It was labelled 'Metsunk' by mirthful GEC executives, who promptly removed all their cash deposits from Barclays. GEC went on to form strategic joint ventures in the EC and US, purchased Ferranti and Plessey, and cruised through the recession, onwards and upwards.

By 1989 the era of the HLT had gone berserk. Two transactions will serve to indicate the sheer hysteria which overtook the market. In the autumn of 1988 the management of RJR-Nabisco, a tobacco and cookies giant originally from North Carolina comprising the former R.J. Reynolds tobacco and National Biscuit companies, announced that the management were organising an MBO at a transaction value of around US$17 billion. In effect, instead of buying an operation out from a larger corporation, the management were now using the MBO structure to buy the whole corporation from its own shareholders! This situation was in fact a complete conflict of interest between the managers and the owners. The New York financier Henry Kravis of the leading MBO firm KKR apparently felt that the RJR-Nabisco management was 'stealing his franchise' to finance this most highly leveraged and highly priced deal of the century. KKR under the direction of its founder Creative Person Jerome Kohlberg had always acted as a 'white knight' rescuer of companies on the wrong end of unwanted hostile bids. Now, however, the firm was considering launching a bid against management's own controversial bid, which itself could only be a hostile bid against the management, but not necessarily against the shareholders' best interests, at least in the theory of the hour. The older Kohlberg disapproved of these Degenerate Person tactics and resigned. The parting was not acrimonious, but it served as a reminder that Creative and Degenerate Persons are not terms expressing black and white, but rather the opposite ends of a gumut of behaviour. For Kohlberg, KKR had switched its balance. Kravis went bravely on and waded in and eventually purchased the entire company for US$25.1 billion, mostly financed by several tiers of debt. A syndicate of two hundred banks – yes, two hundred! – lent US$14.5 billion and received fees of US$325 million. Drexel Burnham provided a US$3.5 billion bridge loan and received fees of US$227 million. These borrowings totalled US$18 billion, but the cash portion of the deal was only US$0.9 billion, as the balance of consideration of US$6.2 billion was in commercial paper, or yet more debt. It only required US$0.9 billion of capital in cash to precipitate a transaction which was valued at twenty-five times that amount! In effect the minuscule level of capital would reap all the profit if and when the buy-out vehicle was sold or refloated on the stock market. A major corporation and thousands of jobs were put at some risk for the sake of a super-profit for the new investors, who were creating no new products or jobs. Ironically, many of the new investors were pension funds of other corporations and organisations. The up-front winners were KKR itself, its professional advisers and bankers who together pocketed a billion dollars in fees. The fees, in fact, were more than the permanent capital introduced. At the closing dinner in New York for four hundred executives, the host quipped 'to think it only needed a billion dollars to get us all together this evening!'

Not to be out-done, the newly formed New York corporate finance boutique of Wasserstein Perella raised an MBO fund from Japanese and American institutions and proceeded to invest most of its fund in a single leveraged buy-out of a supermarket chain. This target company was not based in America, but in Britain, where Wasserstein Perella had no real prior experience. The buy-out vehicle, Isosceles plc, purchased the Gateway foodstore chain for nearly £2 billion in 1989. The transaction went wrong from the start as Gateway's operations could not compete with well organised and conservatively financed chains like Sainsbury, Tesco and Marks & Spencer, even before Gateway took on massive debt of £1.4 billion under the MBO structure. At the time of writing in 1992, Isosceles/Gateway's share capital is probably worthless as the company has negative net worth of £320 million and its trading operations are only kept afloat by the indulgence of its bankers. The 1991 profit scarcely covered the annual interest costs of £160 million. The difference between Henry Kravis and Bruce Wasserstein was one of commercial judgment. RJR-Nabisco had strong cashflows and Kravis did not forget the basic rule of rapidly paying down debt by disposals. He quickly sold off the Del Monte canned and fresh fruit businesses to the Anglo-Turkish Polly Peck, which itself collapsed in 1991. Gateway's cash-flows, however, could scarcely service its debt, let alone provide adequate funds for expansion and a return to capital. The plan to sell off its American Herman's Sporting Goods chain failed completely, as that company's profits were inadequate to attract the right level of bid. The market value of this operation required a provision of £145 million in 1992 to reduce its value to around £50 million.

The point about these transactions, even when they are viable in terms of cashflow as is probably the case for RJR-Nabisco, is that they were not the workings of the capitalist system in the real sense. The capital in these HLT deals was purely 'transactional' money and was not 'investment' money. They were transactions driven by the greed of Degenerate Persons and not the real investment of Creative Persons that develop new businesses, new markets and new jobs. Furthermore, as they involved transactional capital rather than investment capital, they created various distortionary effects in the economy generally. These effects were mainly negative and directly lengthened the ensuing downturn in the early 1990s. Assets which had been unencumbered by debt were now supporting debt for most of their worth, although no new assets had been created. This phenomenon is inflationary, in exactly the same way as borrowing against increasing land value is inflationary. It is inflationary because the former owners of the assets had been paid for them and had recovered their capital at a handsome profit, but they had done this not by the introduction of replacement capital as in a normal stock exchange transaction, for example, but by the creation of debt without any consequent increase in production or productive assets. Secondly, the feverish activity in transactional capital was creating millionaires as never before, and much of the financially-engineered profits from the successful transactions were translated into a further boost to the property markets, both directly by the acquisition of property and by a boom in consumer products. Thirdly, the HLT-mentality triggered the Greed Factor that percolated through all levels of society. A mentality of borrow now to buy into the rising stock market and property markets took firm hold on both sides of the Atlantic. Everyone wanted a piece of the action and the resultant demand really powered through all stages and parts of the economy. The talk of Degenerate Persons was of 'realising shareholder value', which attitude overlooked the fact that investment is essentially a long-term business. It is only speculation that is a short-term business.

Major takeovers were announced almost daily in the 1980s. Some were financed by sound companies and for good strategic industrial reasons. In October 1988, Philip Morris bought the Kraft Food company for US$13.1 billion and in June 1989 Time Inc. bought Warner Communications for US$14 billion to create the largest media company in the world. The British Hanson Trust company made several acquisitions, including US Industries Inc. as well as vast coal reserves in America and Imperial Tobacco plc and Consolidated Goldfields plc in Britain. Other British companies also hit the takeover trail. Some companies with sound management and financing, such as BTR plc (the former British Tyre & Rubber Company) and Williams Holdings plc made a success of several takeovers.

For each logical, sensible and soundly financed takeover put together by Creative Persons, however, there was at least one which was illogical, unnecessary and a monument to the ill-judgment of Degenerate Persons. Many of the same banks and advisers participated in both types. For example, the conservatively run Trustee Savings Bank (TSB), a bank for individuals, decided to launch a £750 million agreed takeover of the Hill Samuel merchant bank just before 'Black Monday' in October 1987. Despite the worldwide stock market crash, TSB insisted on pressing on with its expensive acquisition, for 'reasons of strategic growth'. Upon acquisition, TSB shovelled a billion pounds and more into Hill Samuel to lend out to its corporate customers. These turned out to be mainly property developers who borrowed everything the bank threw at them. It was the peak of the property boom in 1988-89 and the money went straight down the drain. TSB in fact paid twice for its expensive acquisition and Hill Samuel had no real business focus left. Even more unbelievably, British Aerospace paid £287 million cash for Arlington Properties, a developer of business parks, as it had decided that 'property development' was a strategic leg to its aircraft business. It did have a lot of property on its hands as a result of the earlier 'strategic' acquisitions of Rover Cars and Royal Ordnance, but it too bought at the peak in 1989 and effectively lost its investment and business focus. It had engaged reverse thrust instead of forward growth, and its shares fell from over £7 to nearly £1 by 1992.

Four major British public companies also managed to make absurdly priced acquisitions in America that were financed almost entirely by debt. They all paid the ultimate price, insolvency. That archetypal Degenerate Person, the late Robert Maxwell, bought the publisher Macmillan Inc. and the Official Airlines Guide for over US$2 billion on borrowed money, and in the same week! His company, Maxwell Communications, was bust by late 1991. Blue Arrow, a recruitment agency that came from nowhere in the 1980s, launched a record fund-raising exercise in London in 1988 to buy the much larger Manpower Inc. in Milwaukee, for close on £1 billion. The price of Blue Arrow shares collapsed in the after-market, amid allegations that the stock market had been deliberately misled. Similarly, a small construction company from the West Country, Beazer Construction, grew heavily by acquisition in the 1980s to the point where it launched a US $1 billion bid for the Pittsburgh-based Koppers' aggregates business. It was a deal too far, and Hanson Trust plc picked up the pieces in 1991 at a fraction of the cost and in good time for the inevitable and overdue renovation of America's creaking infrastructure. Finally, Ferranti, the electronics concern, bought International Signal and Control of Pennsylvania, but the latter's accounts were fraudulent and included non-existent defence contracts with Pakistan. Ferranti lost £400 million on the deal and was rescued by GEC which purchased some key operations.

A final wild idea was promoted in the summer of 1989 for the pilots and management of United Airlines to buy out their highly cyclical, asset-intensive, debt-strapped business for US$6.8 billion. Luckily for the prospective buyers, which were going to include British Airways as a major investor, an earlier HLT got into financial difficulties and saved everyone the bother and the inevitable losses. Canada's Campeau Corporation, which was also advised by Wasserstein & Perella of Gateway fame, got into serious difficulties in paying the interest on the C$6 billion junk bonds and debt they had raised to acquire Allied & Federated Department Stores in America. Campeau went bust in September, and United Airlines (UAL) could not get its debt money in October, as the Japanese banks pulled back. This failure marked the end of the boom in HLTs and the Dow dropped 190 points on the day, dubbed 'Friday the Thirteenth'. At the time of the UAL collapse Donald Trump, unbelievably, was stumping round the banks to borrow and buy AMR Corporation, the holding company for the well-run American Airlines, for around US$6 billion, but mercifully the banks had stopped listening, or had run out of cash.

The seal was also set for the final collapse in the property market. In January 1990, the Comptroller of the Currency, Mr Robert Clarke, realised that property-lending by banks and S&Ls was so out of control that such lending practices had to be curbed. In February Drexel Burnham filed for bankruptcy after defaulting on over US$100 million in short-term loans. This merchant banker was by far the biggest market maker in the trade in junk bonds and the market collapsed amidst charges of felony and market rigging. At the same time Trump failed to meet interest payments on his massive loans, even without AMR. The Treasury Secretary announced that the S&L fiasco would cost US$300 billion in the 1990s alone, which would push an already alarming Federal deficit even higher. As 1990 developed it became clear that the economy would not achieve the soft landing that Alan Greenspan, the Federal Reserve Chairman, was hoping for. By November he had to announce that the economy was in a 'meaningful downturn' but he concluded that 'recession may still be avoidable'! It was not until January 1991 that the White House conceded that the economy was already in recession. By this time twenty-eight states in the Union faced budget deficits, and on 6 January the Bank of New England had to be taken over by regulators, as it was bust. The bank had been brought down by the collapse in the property market. Developers and owners defaulted on their loans by simply handing back the keys of hundreds of properties. Suddenly it was clear that banks and S&Ls across the country were caught in a near terminal squeeze. In his State of the Union address President Bush still managed to say at the end of that month that growth would be resumed soon, but by now the banking and S&L crisis had been triggered by the biggest collapse in property values the world had ever seen. The Federal deficit was rising remorselessly. At this point the sheer paucity of economic thinking was laid bare. The new President had already reneged on his 1988 promise of 'no new taxes' in 1990, but now his government believed that its only option was to slash interest rates and let the dollar 'go to hell in a handcart', effectively devaluing the massive level of external debt and with cheap money grabbing whatever work there was left in a recessionary world.

Meanwhile in Britain the early 1990s saw the property markets start collapsing, just as in Texas and in New England, as interest rates rose, tenants disappeared and rentals dropped. The collapse of the Canary Wharf project in London's docklands was not the only major collapse. Even in the heart of the City of London, which had never ever experienced a significant collapse in property prices during several centuries, vast losses were incurred as demand dried up and the market became a buyer's paradise and a seller's nightmare. At Paternoster Square, adjoining St Paul's Cathedral, an Anglo-Japanese consortium invested a total of £215 million to acquire an out-of-date 850,000-square-feet office block. The redevelopment has not yet started, but by August 1992 the offices were 80% vacant and were valued by experts (advising the *Daily Mail* newspaper) at only £40 million, indicating a loss of over 80%. The Alban Gate development in nearby London Wall cost a major British property company £225 million, but was 90% empty and was valued by the same experts at only £125 million. (Subsequently it let 50% in September 1992 but at an undisclosed rental.) The Ludgate development in front of St Paul's Cathedral cost £200 million, but was 85% empty and was valued by these experts again at only £100 million. These whacking losses quickly wiped out the capital invested and hit the banks. Nor was there any better news in the residential market, where prices were off their peak by 30% and still falling, as annual repossessions approached 85,000 dwellings. The number of borrowers overdue with mortgage repayments exceeded a further 330,000. In the autumn of 1992 substantial further drops in property values will be inevitable unless interest rates decline quite rapidly, following Britain's detachment from the ERM.

As the stock and property markets went into reverse, so the stockbroking and estate agency firms that had been acquired in the rush to buy in the mid-1980s went into decline. About 150,000 jobs disappeared on Wall Street and about half that number in the City of London. There were still about thirty securities houses trading in London in the summer of 1992, with only enough volume to support half-a-dozen. The mighty Prudential Corporation sold off the estate agency business it had acquired only a few years before, for a

Insert 5

Who Needs the Treasury Computer? – Part Two

Markets can be merciful: just as UAL and AMR, with the help of BA and Mr Trump respectively, were about to be submerged in new debt equivalent to six times their capital, Friday the Thirteenth intervened and closed the runways. How Mr Robert Campeau must have wished his highly leveraged takeover of Federated had been similarly stalled before take-off in 1988.

Markets can be merciless: try as the former UK Chancellor did to follow the high-powered Deutschemark, his all-important 3DM/£1 level was breached – no doubt permanently – as he discovered that a Central European Bank already existed: it's called the Bundesbank. However, his strategy was saved – temporarily – by, unbelievably, the UAL buy-out collapse. Sterling promptly rose against the mighty dollar, until his resignation.

It is time for quoted and unquoted markets to settle down and focus on the forthcoming recession, even if it proves to be mild. At this stage it would appear that housebuilding, furnishings, other non-food retailers and motor cars are leading the downward cycle, with manufacturers supplying these industries set to follow.

Source: *Newsletter for Select Industries Trust*, November 1989.

Footnote: The Treasury even failed to forecast the depth of the recession throughout 1990, or its severity in 1991. As the Treasury saw recovery in Autumn 1991, the real economy was actually plunging lower.

cumulative loss of over £200 million. Then the British insurance industry found itself staring at a potential £2 billion loss on new-style policies granted to insure property values to mortgagee companies, many of them rashly written at the top of the boom. And for good measure losses at the Lloyds' insurance market, which was scandal-ridden throughout the 1970s, compounded by inefficiency during the 1980s, produced losses of over £3 billion between 1989 and 1991 for its Names, or the individuals shouldering the risks. These losses further depressed the housing market, consumer demand and confidence, as many Names were forced to sell their homes and other assets.

The boom of the Greed Decade took place on the back of rising property values and it ended when those values went into freefall, caused by natural market forces. The boom in property values attracted a massive availability of credit, which credit was also used to change the ownership of industrial assets without adding anything to real investment in the companies concerned. It is unlikely that anyone alive today will see such excess in financial markets again in their lifetime. Never before was so much money squandered by so few people to achieve so little, with so many professional advisers pocketing such large fees. The result is a large unpaid bill in debt and interest. The property markets and many MBOs, together with several of the financial institutions that funded these sectors, no longer survive to pay it.

It is said that there are two kinds of idiot, the one that gets out in time and the one that doesn't. President Reagan, a prototypical escapee who could always read the lines that were written for him, got out at the top and donated Vice-President Bush as his successor, but Bush was always his own economic epitaph. Prime Minister Thatcher stayed on too long, or not long enough depending on your view of her successor, John Major, who won an amazing electoral victory in April 1992 against all the odds but has not yet begun to win an economic victory of any sort at all. In the 1980s the bulls and bears that got in and out in time made money, but the pigs went broke.

10

Taking Stock in the 1990s

How did the 1980s, which promised so much, end in a worldwide slump? That is the question that must be answered in order to set the agenda for macro-economic management and restructuring in the 1990s. The fundamental problem is that the relationship between the two primary factors of production, land and labour, is not sufficiently recognised and catered for in the English-speaking capitalist economies. The tribe on its homelands has none of the problems discussed in the previous chapter. It is true that it does not enjoy the enormous benefits thrown up by capitalism either, but it is also clear that capitalism has got to re-examine its basic structure, methods and ways of doing business. In particular the incidence of taxation on the two primary factors of production must be radically overhauled, before industry dies of financial and fiscal starvation and before another boom in property values and attendant borrowings brings the financial system nearer collapse.

The flotsam and jetsam of the 1980s is all around for us to see. Polly Peck, Bank of Credit & Commerce, Coloroll, Levitt Group, Maxwell Communications, British & Commonwealth, Mountleigh Properties and a host of other British Companies have gone under. In America bank and S&L failures are legion. Pan-Am, American West and Continental no longer fly or are in insolvency, and TWA is about to crash-land. GPA Group, the Irish-based aircraft leasing business, is struggling to raise capital and to defer firm orders for new equipment. Wang Computers, Prime Computers and scores of other computer firms are bust. Hundreds of property developers on both sides of the Atlantic are either bust or bleeding and bandaged, while industry no longer needs their creations. The list is headed by Olympia & York and Trump in Toronto and New York, but closely followed by Britain's largest private company, Heron Corporation, which also succumbed to the lure of the 'Big Apple'. Even Britain's S & W Berisford, which owned the country's second largest sugar business, managed to lose £120 million on property deals in Manhattan, and was largely dismembered. Burton Group, the menswear retailer, lost even more in shopping developments back in its native Britain, but is just about surviving, when it could have been thriving. The rest of Britain's walking wounded are concentrated in London and the South East, including Brent Walker, Stanhope, Rosehaugh, Regalian, Speyhawk and

Greycoat, to mention just a few that went public with their shares and are now public with their debt problems. In November 1991, banks in Britain had lent a staggering £41.5 billion to commercial property companies alone, compared to £17.5 billion in real terms in the previous boom-bust peak in 1974-75. It is crystal clear that the structure of our Anglo-American economic system resembles a battlefield where property slugs it out with industry to the detriment of both, as well as to the banks and their customers.

Table 5: Britain's Commercial Property Lending, November 1991

£0,000,000,000s (billions)

	£ Bn		£ Bn
British clearing banks	17.6	Barclays	5.4
Japanese banks	4.6	Nat-West	2.5
American banks	2.2	Lloyds	2.3
Other overseas banks	10.4	Midland	1.6
British merchant banks	2.7	Other clearers	5.4
Other British banks	2.4	Other banks	5.1
	£41.5 Bn		£22.3 Bn

Note: If other property-related loans are included, the total rises to £63.5 billion at 31 December 1991.

Source: *Bank of England quarterly statistics*.

At the end of February 1992 British Bankers' Association figures showed total loans of £261.7 billion. Nomura Securities' banking analyst's opinion was that around 75% of this total was secured on property, one way or another. In physical terms, between 1989 and 1991, about 15 million of new office space was added to the City of London's stock compared with about 5 million square feet in the 1972-74 boom. It is estimated that in the autumn of 1992 there are approximately 12 million square feet of office space available in the City, out of a total of approximately 60 million square feet, which will create an overhang for around three to five years, forcing rents down by up to 50% or more between 1989 and 1992-94.

Not a single government or school of economic thought has put forward a plan for recovery and better management in the 1990s that has captured the imagination of the public as even credible, in the sense of it inspiring confidence that it stands a chance of succeeding. If left to itself, there is little doubt that the world economy might slowly, very slowly, revive on the back of the natural cycle in much the same pattern as from the previous recession of 1980-81. It will undoubtedly take longer as consumer demand, the major engine of recovery, is blunted by the excessive levels of private-sector debt in America, Britain and Japan, while Germany is also mired in debt, but of a different kind, arising from the costs of reunification. The British government's economic policy was to do just that, to wait for the recovery. Until it came, the only economic policy that it had adopted was to leave sterling in the ERM, guaranteeing historically high real interest rates until inflation was reduced to the unlikely level of zero. From 1972 to 1977, real interest rates in Britain were negative, but from 1981 they have been positive as a consequence. In 1992 they were positive by over 6% until withdrawal from the ERM in September. The government's approach took no account of issues such as unemployment, asset deflation, bankruptcy, dwindling exports and investment, a growing PSBR and a continuing decline in the manufacturing base. When recovery does eventually dawn, the economy will simply create a weaker profile of the 1980s, with the Treasury no doubt boosting the economy when it is already too late, just as in 1986-88, producing yet another recession. Where is the sense in that?

The first part of this approach, of letting recovery come through on its own, is not without merit, now that Britain is out of the ERM and in charge of its own destiny once again. The 1982-83 recovery started with the industrial restocking and investment cycle during 1981-82, and then consumer spending, at two-thirds of GDP, took over in 1982-83.

Table 6: The 1982-83 Recovery in Britain

Growth Rates	1981 (Q2) – 1982 (Q2)	1982 (Q2) – 1983 (Q2)
GDP	2.2%	3.1%
Consumer spending	0%	4.9%
Spending on durables	−1.3%	22.9%
New car registrations	0.5%	17.1%
Real personal incomes	0.9%	2.3%
Manufacturing output	1.9%	1.1%
Government spending	0%	3.2%
Investment	4.5%	3.2%

Source: *Economic Trends Annual Supplement*, 1992.

10. Taking Stock in the 1990s

The surge in consumer and durables spending and new car purchases in 1982-83 sustained the impetus started by industrial investment in 1981-1982. The restocking, investment and consumer-demand cycles may produce a repeat recovery performance in 1992-93, but there is a distinct feeling in the economic air – but not in the Treasury computer – that time is of the essence. The long cycle of 90 years has turned down. North Sea oil is running out. Manufacturing is dropping below a self-sustaining mass. Britain may only have one further decade to get its economy into better shape. There is no time for the crass errors of Degenerate Persons now.

It is already clear that the imbalance in the British and American economies between declining industry and the property boom-and-bust cycle is a losing strategy. The key lies in taxation, along with other related measures, to restore the balance. It is clear that the cost of local government has got to be shifted back to local resources. In other words, those who receive local services have got to pay for local services. They cannot pay for the local services they receive if they are over-taxed centrally. The Conservative Party's plan to reduce central government taxation was a great success but its attempts to reorganise local government finances in the 1980s were a fiasco. The community charge was meant to make everyone of age pay for local services, but many households paid less than under the old rating system while others paid more and the total of local taxation actually went down. The people objected to a tax on their heads with such ferocity that it spelled the end for Mrs Thatcher. The council tax starting in 1993-94 is merely the same old lady of rateable values dressed up in a new frock decorated with hoops to represent valuation bands of fixed taxation levels. It does nothing to redress the incidence of taxation on industry, and it too will have to go, the quicker the better. In fact it would be better simply to cancel it and run the existing taxes for another year and then introduce Community Value Tax. The Conservatives have spent four years on the issue of funding local authorities and have walked all round the problem without solving it.

It is also clear that deregulation of the financial services market has been an unmitigated disaster and a primary factor in booming property values and inflation. The City developed a casino-like atmosphere in the 1980s which spilled over into all types of excess. The level of fraud and financial scandals, together with major accounting failures, reached an all-time high. The integrity and self-discipline procedures of the professions failed in too many instances, through cover-ups, delays, lack of expertise and sheer incompetence. The Serious Fraud Office managed to obtain convictions against executives and associates of Guinness, but no City professional was pursued successfully. Similarly convictions were obtained in the Blue Arrow trial at a loss to the taxpayer of £30 million, but were overturned on appeal on technicalities. The reform of fraud trials was recommended by Lord Roskill's report, but the government rejected it. The establishment of Self-Regulatory Organisations has been an expensive farce, as the Maxwell scandal has proven. The BOBOs could spot a wrong 'un a mile away and had their own ways of dealing with sharp practice. A return of the old standards would be welcome, and that can only come from the top. More heads need to roll in future and be seen to roll in cases of proven fraud. Lord Roskill's report, which recommended trial of fraud by a panel comprising a judge, an accountant and a lawyer, rather than by a jury who cannot follow the technical evidence, was eminently sensible. It should be implemented without delay, as integrity is the City's principal asset. In 1992, the debate on corporate governance has at last started, when Creative Persons on the Cadbury Committee published their first report on the role of non-executive directors and the issues of directors' pay and the appointment of auditors. It is vital that this initiative maintains its momentum and clearly defined standards become widely accepted and implemented.

There is not the slightest doubt in any quarter that inflation will bankrupt the world if left unchecked, but thankfully this issue is now widely perceived as a fundamental economic necessity. There is progress on that front in the short term as far as Britain is concerned, even if the government has no plans of its own in place to prevent a repeat performance of double-digit inflation in the 1990s, except to raise interest rates again, and thereby raise bankruptcies, currently running at over 1,000 per week, home repossessions, unemployment, central government costs and the PSBR. 'Not much of an economic policy, that one ain't, and not one up with which the British people will easily put,' I hear you mutter darkly. The government has got to stop just standing there and go find a policy. It has got to address the problem at home as its first priority. It is time to kick-start the Chancellor!

Abroad, meanwhile, Britain wants to promote free trade in Europe and between Europe and the rest of the world, without sacrificing its national interests to unelected Eurocrats in Brussels or Strasbourg telling everyone what's best for them. The latest nonsense involves a chemical compound that is found in bird food which makes flamingoes go pink. It has been banned by the EC Commission, but its withdrawal reduced the flamingo reproduction rate, whereas the ban does not extend to its inclusion in popular pink German sausages. I ask you! Specifically, Britain is a key member of the EC, but this does not mean that it has to lose the strength of its traditional ties with the

English-speaking world, with America and The Commonwealth. In fact Britain wants to reaffirm its role in the world, based on domestic prosperity, much as it did in the reigns of Elizabeth I or George III, and from within the EC. For example, while Germany is fretting over its pink sausages, Britain should be warning the world about the threat of economic collapse in the former USSR. The winds of change blow through the Brandenburg Gate, and there is a lot of it about to the East. At the G7 summit in London in the summer of 1991 President Gorbachev asked for massive loans, but his Business Plan did not add up and his loan application was refused. As it was HM Treasury that allegedly demanded a 'Peace Dividend' after the collapse of the USSR in 1990, we should all take the threat very seriously indeed, because it has not gone away. Russian GDP is forecast to fall by a massive 10% in 1993 and payments to suppliers in Poland, East Germany and Scandinavia have stopped. The Russian rouble is entering hyperinflation. (Don't they teach history any more?) Three Russian conventional submarines have just been sold to Iran to raise cash, but the armoured equipment being produced in the West to move the arsenal of Soviet nuclear missiles will not be deployed for several years. The G7 has got to formulate an economic plan to help the economy of the former USSR, centred on the idea of bartering co-operation and assistance on industrialisation in exchange for those things which Russia has in abundance, namely metals, minerals and the finest submarines, aircraft and space equipments in the world. If the banks were not bogged down at home with their property loans, they too could finance the exporters and the barter process. Britain should not let Europe and the Americans become introverted on their own problems. The DTI announced in Moscow in September 1992 the issue of a government-backed credit for £250 million, which is not even a drop in an ocean. The threat of the consequences of disintegration of the former USSR economies could be turned by the vision of Creative Persons on both sides into the biggest economic opportunity going. For example, the former USSR's incredible Oscar Class nuclear submarine technology could be economically harnessed to bulk transport of the world's trade, at underwater dash speeds of twice the speed of surface ships and a fraction of the cost.

The combined output of the English-speaking world is about 40% of World GDP, whereas the EC is only about 24%. British industry enjoys traditional stamping grounds in America and The Commonwealth. The common language and shared cultural characteristics mean that British companies will continue to look at the world opportunities, beyond just the EC. It is clear that overseas investment will be mainly in America rather than the EC, given the latter's restrictions on takeovers. The total 'visible' deficit on trade with the EC since 1981 amounted to £69 billion, and the 'invisibles' have only been about equal. Britain's EC budgetary contributions, 60% of which goes to the CAP, have amounted to £13.1 billion. From 1981-90 the UK balance of payments current account total deficit was £81 billion, equivalent to its EC deficit. Moreover Britain is just as likely to receive inward investment from both America and Japan, particularly post-devaluation. Britain really scores here from the openness of its capital markets. Inward investment from America brings technology, and the Japanese are providing an object lesson in industrial renaissance, management, productivity and quality. For both these countries Britain remains a viable platform within the EC from which to target its 320 million consumers.

A nagging question keeps posing itself about (West) Germany. What have they got that Britain has not got, and vice versa. What lessons are there to learn? Britain owns over 35% of the top 500 quoted companies in Europe, which would indicate that it should be the economic leader of the EC. On 13 January 1992 the *Financial Times* survey, European Top 500, showed Royal Dutch/Shell, British Telecom, Glaxo, British Petroleum and Unilever plc/NV as occupying the first five positions. The market capitalisation of UK plc representatives was US$737.9 billion compared to Germany's US$251.1 billion. For example, Britain has a financial services sector second to none, despite the bank's current exposure to property. Britain has the four London clearing banks, the three main Scottish banks, the Ulster bank, three other major banks and half-a-dozen top merchant banks. Germany has three main banks, only one of which, Deutsche Bank, has a significant international presence, including its ownership of Britain's Morgan Grenfell. Germany has a strong insurance sector, led by its single biggest company, Allianz, but Britain has a much greater capacity. Britain's retail sector is, perversely perhaps, the best in Europe. In electronics, the German Siemens, AEG and Nixdorf are mightier perhaps than GEC/Plessey, Racal and Thorn/EMI. In energy, however, Britain has Shell Transport, B.P., Burmah Castrol, British Gas, Enterprise Oil and Lasmo, compared to Germany's Veba, their own coalfields and their heavy dependence on the Dutch Groningen gas fields. (Think of what that natural resource does to the site value of Holland!) Britain's agriculture is the most efficient and least subsidised in Europe, and it has major food and drinks companies like Associated British Foods, Allied-Lyons, Cadbury-Schweppes, Guinness and a whole host of brewers, Northern Foods, United Biscuits, Unilever and many others, that compare favourably with German producers. Germany may have the biggest media company in the EC in Bertelsmann A.G., but Britain has a world profile in publishing, newspapers and TV with companies like Reed International, Granada, Reuters and even the BBC's television exports, which capitalise on the universality of the English language. British Airways betters Lufthansa, and Trust House Forte, Bass Holiday Inns and Queens Moat Houses' hotel groups have more coverage than any indigenous German group. There are many British engineering groups that have substantial operations in Germany, such as Redland with building products and GKN with motor components. The Germans have a large pharmaceutical and medical supplies sector, but Britain's Glaxo is the EC's largest single manufacturing company, not forgetting ICI Bio, Smith & Nephew, [Smithkline] Beecham, Fisons and Wellcome. Germany certainly has nothing to compare with Britain's acquisitive multi-national conglomerates like Hanson Trust, BTR and Williams Holdings.

Where Germany wins out is in efficient mass production, particularly in heavy engineering, steel production, motor vehicle and consumer durables manufacturing. Volkswagen is the EC's largest car producer, Mercedes makes the best trucks and Germany still has Audi, BMW and Porsche. Britain's motor industry only seems to have a future under foreign management, particularly Japanese. (As the Lex column of the *Financial Times* remarked on 29 September 1992, 'The Japanese investment in Britain looks increasingly smart', following devaluation.) Germany scores heavily too in bulk chemicals, with companies like Bayer, Hoechst and BASF. Its banks invest in and agree industry's financial plans and targets, and then industry delivers. *Befehl ist Befehl* – 'an order is an order'. Industries tend to be led by giants which know their strategic aims and then management executes the orders from above with legendary Teutonic efficiency. In Britain, for example, the system depends on a Hanson Trust or GEC threatening a takeover for some top management teams to focus. The two systems are quite different, reflecting the character of each nation.

Germany also has a much larger 'domestic' market, domestic in the sense that the Germanic peoples in Europe are more than double the Anglo-Saxon population. In addition countries like Switzerland, Italy, Austria, [Eastern] France, Holland, Denmark, Poland, East Germany, Hungary, Czechoslovakia and even Russia fall within her natural sphere of influence. The English-speaking family is more far-flung and spread around the globe. Germany's market opportunities are on her doorstep and favour mass production and support the German tendency to keep moving up-market with better and better products as a natural migration. This cohesion in the German industrial powerhouse is held together by three important factors. After WW2, the British (no less!) advised that only one trade union should represent each industry and Germany was spared the endless demarcation disputes that bedeviled British industry in the 1960s and 1970s. Secondly, the concept of *Mitbestimmung* or 'worker co-determination' was introduced into all companies employing over 2,000 workers. Representatives of the unions, management and workers, both blue- and white-collar, sat on the Supervisory Board of the company and so everyone knew the game plan. More important, the *Betriebsverfassungsgesetz*, or Works' Constitution Act, set up Works Councils at virtually every place of work, from the biggest plants down to SMEs and even to a handful of employees. These apolitical councils make decisions on every type of condition of employment and working conditions generally, other than pay, and their decisions are binding on unions, workers and management. This process, which is beyond the influence of politicians, defuses or settles disputes and averts strikes by forestalling them. British management has a lot to learn from the German (and Japanese) examples.

The advantage of the German structure is that their vast number of SMEs supplying the industrial majors are themselves similarly disciplined by orders from above. The presence of banks on the shareholders' register also helps spread the risk of new investments and lends confidence to the entrepreneurs. So the whole locomotive gathers a momentum of its own and the accent is on planning, production, quality, design, delivery and service. Germany, however, is also the land of myths and fairytales, not to mention propaganda. The problem for the German mentality is with the unexpected, when a piece of bent, rusty old iron like East Germany is left lying on the track and the whole train, now charging along with money supply growth at 9%, gets derailed. This could never happen in Britain as half the train would not have reached the departure point on time anyway. In the bit of the train that did depart, there would have been a bright boffin on board who would have spotted and dealt with the threat in the nick of time. In WW2 the Spitfire took 13,000 production hours per copy, with Joe and Jane working in two old Morris car factories and with Merlin engine components being produced to a tolerance of a thou' on belt-driven lathes. The ME109 took only 4,000 production hours per copy. George Mitchell's creation, however, was far more versatile than Willy Messerschmitt's in combat.

But the key issue is nearer to home. It is clear that the incidence of taxation has got to be moved back from industry and on to property values. It is only equitable that what the community has created for itself in the form of community value it should take back again to itself to pay for community expenditure. It is quite absurd that industry pays to remove the householder's dustbin! The need is to have local services paid for by local beneficiaries. There is a question as to whether state education should be included at the local level. It is the biggest local expense by far and it should probably be dealt with by central government. I hesitate at this point, as I am not seeking to address the political issue of who should set and control educational standards. I am only interested in the issue of what is economically and fiscally fair. By leaving this enormous budget item with local government, however, it remains the lure which attracts central government into taking the baited trap of acknowledging an obligation to fund local expenditure in the first place. For this reason alone it would be sensible to move education back to central government's budget. *The United Kingdom National Accounts, 1991* discloses that the total of Local Authorities' budgets for 1990 was £57.4 billion, of which £52.5 billion was current expenditure (see Table 7). Of this £57.4 billion nearly £20.4 billion was for education, after including the cost of educational grants. Although education is delivered locally, it is a central decision to provide state eduction. All education, both state and private, is paid for ultimately by the public, by taxes or out of income.

Nevertheless the British character has preferred to mould a mixed economy as regards medical, educational and other essential services, but it seems that there is no logical or compelling argument why the National Health Service should be a central government expense and state education should be a local government expense. So let us move education back to central government, for economic purposes. That leaves a £37 billion local government budget to fund. Rents, interest and other income generate £5.5 billion, so there is £31.5 billion to fund before a 'current surplus' is created. Why a current surplus of £4.9 billion is required is not clear. The danger in any organisation is that money left over is always spent. Finally, the balance of local taxation between residences, whose householders have a local vote, and business premises, whose owners and tenants are not locally enfranchised, should also reflect site values or an appropriate calculation of annual community values. It is inequitable that businesses pay a disproportionate amount of local taxes, which must adversely affect economic growth and therefore employment (see Insert 3).

Table 7: Local Authorities: 1990 Current Account
£0,000,000,000 (billions)

Receipts

Current grants from central government	38.0
Rates + Community Charge	13.9
Rents, interest and other income	5.5
	57.4

Expenditure

Education, including grants	20.4
Public order and safety	6.8
Social security (mainly 'personal social services')	5.7
Housing and community amenity	3.0
Recreational and cultural affairs	2.3
General public services	2.0
Transport and communication	1.9
Subsidies	.6
Rent rebates and allowances	4.5
Debt interest	5.3
	52.5
Current Surplus	4.9
	57.4

Source: *United Kingdom National Accounts, 1991* (Abstract from Section 8).

It is a great shame that when Mrs Thatcher reduced the higher band of income tax from 60% to 40% in 1988 her government did not use the opportunity to load local property taxes at the same time, so as to achieve a fiscally neutral result for taxpayers. In fact under her government general government expenditure as a percentage of money GDP fell by 15% from 45.75% in 1980-81 to 39.75% in 1990-91. (Something has alerted the author's corrupt data bogey sensor here: that does not seem quite right. The tax reduction was surely a bigger percentage drop than 15%? In fact, on looking at the small print under Table 2A.1 on page 16 of the 1992-93 *Red Book*, we learn that the GDP figure has itself been 'adjusted to remove the distortion caused by the abolition of domestic rates', no less! – the very quarry we were after. Another Treasury fiddle that ends up fooling its creator – see what I mean about the problems of corrupt data?) Mrs Thatcher appeared to have been blinded from the real issue of local taxation by two of her own *idées fixes*. The idea of a property-owning democracy appealed to her householder instincts, as well as securing the likelihood of more Conservative Party votes. Instead of realising that the greater part of a particular property's value attaches to the community value, however, she determined to tax the people in the building rather than the site on which it stood. The number of residents can never be ascertained with accuracy, but the site's community value can never be hidden from view.

This missed opportunity was tragic in its consequences. The fiscal reduction (which we now know was greater than 15% of GDP), coupled with lower interest rates in 1988, introduced when the Treasury forgot to look at M0, caused the final vault in the property boom which has caused so much pain and so many losses since. At the same time it may come to be seen that the 'unearned' bonanza of North Sea oil appears to have been squandered from an industrial perspective, which loss really is a national tragedy. Meanwhile industry trudges on paying the bulk of the nation's taxes, and property values slump, weighed down with a debt burden that would and should never have been there in a properly balanced economy, balanced that is between industry and property.

The proper tax on property would have removed the heady values that charmed the banks into lending so much money on property. From the 1988 tax reductions at the height of the short cycle of nine years, it is only four and a half years to the bottom of the short cycle in the autumn of 1992. What is clear is that with the 1992-93 forecast PSBR rising to £28.1 billion, and no doubt over £40 billion in 1993-94, Britain's taxes must be raised. If they are not raised, inflation will rise as a result of the increasing level of debt and demand. Needless to say, the Treasury has probably not yet realised taxes must rise or, if it has, is saying nothing while it desperately seeks to rein in public spending. What is also probable is that the Treasury's only perception will be to raise income tax back up again towards 60%, as it fails to appreciate that the incidence of such a tax increase will fall on industry. This is a critical decision for the UK economy, as the opportunity is approaching to put the inevitable tax increase, when it does come, back on to community values and not on to industry, by raising local revenues from a new community value tax instead, and in effect redressing Mrs Thatcher's 1988 missed opportunity. The problem is, quite simply, how to prove to the authorities the wisdom of this approach and also the fact that there really are site values that can yield the necessary revenues back to the community.

As long ago as 1973, the Land Institute of London carried out a detailed analysis of the site valuation of properties in Whitstable on the North Kent coastline. This town (of 25,000 inhabitants in 1973) is famous for its oyster beds but is otherwise unremarkable from an economic point of view. Consequently its site value is undoubtedly below the national average, which average would include the much greater site values of Britain's cities and industrial heartlands. The study was inspired by a government Green Paper, *The Future Shape of Local Government Finance*, published in July 1971, which stated that 'the objective of new local taxes is not to increase the overall level of taxation; it is to find a means by which a greater part of local authority expenditure can be met out of income raised locally by the authorities themselves, and a correspondingly smaller part therefore met from government grants paid for out of national taxation'. These central government grants (before moving education back to central government) are still the second largest item in the budget twenty years later and stand at £52.5 billion per annum! The Green Paper stated that 'the main arguments put forward in favour of site value rating are that the economic rent of the site is created not by the owner but by the community, so that it is right for the community to recover a share of this value by taxing it... unlike the present system [of Local Authority Rates], site value rating would not tax – and hence discourage – improvements' (para 2.72). The Green Paper is of course referring to community value as defined.

The Whitstable report concluded that the rateable value of the town under the old rating system was £2,703,667 in 1973, but that under site value rating would have been £3,695,589, an increase of 37%. This conclusion shows that rateable values of developed sites had actually fallen behind just the site value element, although the report declared that much of this increase related to land not liable at that time to fall within the rating provisions, which nevertheless had a site value. Taking this surplus of £1 million at 1973 prices per 25,000 population, based on a total population of 57.4 million, would indicate a national surplus from site value rating over the old rateable values of £2,296 million. Allowing for inflation in the Housing Index between 1974 and 1991 of 857.1%, the surplus in real terms would amount to nearly £20 billion in 1991. Even allowing for the inconclusive nature of the Whitstable study, it nevertheless reveals the probability of a massive under-taxation of community values. The fact that this amount of taxation may not have been levied on actual annual site values – that is, on the community's expansion,

128

which directly and naturally enhances land values – means that any such shortfall in taxation has fallen mainly on industry or been financed by an increase in National Debt. The fact that this unnecessary fiscal penalisation of industry has probably gone on for forty-seven years since WW2 may go a long way to explaining industry's real decline and the very real growth in property values, particularly houses. A massive imbalance in our national resources is staring at us and calling for a fundamental reappraisal of our economic priorities and fiscal restructuring of our national finances. Anyone who lived through the 1980s in Britain and America and who did not see that we were mainly Degenerate Persons disregarding real investment in industry, but enjoying a credit-driven property and takeover binge instead, either had their eyes shut or was living in a cardboard city. Indeed one of the main perceived benefits of site value rating was that land held out of use would be brought on to the open market, thus forcing rents down, which could only be beneficial to inflation and a potential opportunity for new industry and for the unemployed. And the report also found that site value rating was easier to administer and less cumbersome than the old rating valuation method.

The Whitstable Report was important as it was the first attempt to measure site or community value in Britain. It also laid bare the romantic assumption and assertion of the nineteenth-century Liberal economists that site value rating could remove all taxes from industry, as fondly claimed by the 'single taxers' – it certainly cannot do that! That it may be enough to swing the economy into better balance as regards the incidence of taxation is justification itself. To be fair to those century-old economists, however, the economy they were addressing was very different from that of the end of the second millennium. Since WW2 Britain has built a mixed economy, including a National Health Service and a Welfare State, offering social security and unemployment benefits to all. In addition the defence bill has soared, with the introduction of an air force, missiles, electronic warfare and other expensive equipment. The mixed economy and the growth of the defence industry into the nation's largest manufacturing sector have changed the size and shape of the economy. For example, the health service is a major expense (see Table 2) funded out of central taxation. It becomes a major customer of industry too when it purchases buildings, equipment, pharmaceuticals, medical preparations, vehicles, power and running services. Industry benefits directly from this major 'new' customer, so that the drug companies and other suppliers themselves expand and buy buildings, equipment, vehicles and the rest. It is the same with the defence industry. In effect a considerable part of taxes on industry is recycled into finance for industry's customers. To this extent it is inconceivable that any form of land value taxation could begin to fund a modern economy like Britain's.

The era of those gallant 'single taxers' has long since gone. Their vital legacy is the issue of the optimum balance in the incidence of taxation. What must be borne in mind is that a considerable portion of the two payroll taxes, income tax and social security, which amounted in 1991-92 to £96.3 billion, were not really taxation that stayed with central government, but were a financial recycling mechanism to fund the nation's two largest industries (other than unemployment!), namely the health and defence industries that cost £47.7 billion (see Table 2). Oh, the problems of corrupt data: for now we must watch our use of words as well. What is called income tax on individuals has turned out to be an employment tax which is partly a subvention to transfer money to other industries and partly an employment tax to pay for central government costs. The subvention element to other industries creates employment and the taxation element deters employment. The social security tax is exactly the same in effect, only it is calculated differently, so it has a different name. In case you think it pays for unemployment 'benefits' – wrong word again, should be 'costs' – do not forget that in 1992-93 the government is planning to borrow £28.1 billion from all those 'nasty foreigners' who speculated in sterling and devalued it in September 1992, just before the borrowing really got going. This borrowing is to pay for unemployment, but the government is not clearly telling the taxpayers, or rather the borrowers. Now, how on earth the Treasury Mandarins feed all that into their computer without producing enough GIGO to feed the whole of Italy, the Lord alone knows!

It is time to start again. Scrap the whole rotten edifice. Take Hamlet's advice: 'Reform it altogether.'

11

Blueprint for Britain's Target 2000

The issue of the hour in September 1992 appears to be Britain's membership of the ERM and the future of the EMU in the EC. Britain joined the ERM in October 1990 at a mid-rate of 2.95 Deutschemarks to the pound. It joined at the wrong time and at the wrong rate for the wrong reasons. (Someone actually said this at the time, but they did not work at the Treasury.) The effect has been to maintain real interest rates and prolong the recession. The damage that has been done cannot now be reversed. Prime Minister Major, who took Britain into the ERM as Chancellor of the Exchequer, found himself in the same awkward spot as Macbeth – he was steeped in red ink so far that to go on was just as bad as going back. Luckily for him, the fluctuating fortunes of politics has given him a break and forced a realignment within the ERM. Although Britain left the ERM on 16 September 1992, the ERM whirlpool will still have a major influence on sterling and economic policy, even if Britain never rejoins the ERM, which seems unlikely. Maastricht is trying to do some of the right strategic things, but too early in the process of creating a true common market. The foreign exchange markets also know something the Euro-fanatics have overlooked. The future of the British economy will be governed by events in America, and to a lesser extent in The Commonwealth, as much as by the EC. Britain is in a unique position, both geographically and strategically. She must be in the EC as a free trade partner, but EMU is not a necessity in the same way that it is for France, with its dependence on the CAP and Germany as its main trading partner. There is simply no sound reason why monetary union should take precedence over, for example, harmonisation of tax regimes and tax rates, which are a far greater distortion on prices and borrowing and therefore indirectly on exchange rates.

For example, the famous Tattersall's of Newmarket has announced its intention to move to Ireland where VAT on thoroughbred sales is only 3.5% compared to the UK's 17.5%, and to France's 5%. Guess which country is not going to win the Derby in the brave new EC of 1993. (Treasury reaction? 'Politically not possible to set a lower VAT rate for such an activity, sport of kings and all that.' Get away! Surely, we are meant to be joining the *common* market, not creating more unemployment in Newmarket, for heaven's sake!) As it is, in September 1992, Britain has the fastest rate of decline in inflation in Europe and has endured two years of recession and most of the bad debts are out in the open. Germany, whose currency heads the ERM, is experiencing rising interest rates at nearly 10%, as the financing requirement to subsidise East Germany approaches 150 billion Deutschemarks for 1992-93. It has rising bankruptcies and has been entering recession since mid-1992. The Americans have reduced prime rate to 6% and the short-term discount rate to 3%, and sterling is caught in the crossfire between the Deutschemark and the dollar. The high German interest rates are sucking in funds to finance reunification and the ERM spreads the cost to the other EC members through high interest rates. But Britain's base rate has already come down from 15%, where it was stuck for over a year until autumn 1990, when it finally dropped 1% to 14%. ERM was definitely hurting as far as Britain was concerned and was certainly not working. Britain found itself contributing to the rebuilding of the German economy for the third time this century while in the ERM, but is now mercifully free once again to pursue its own policy.

From a purely economic point of view, leaving aside political pressures, the pragmatic approach for Britain in Europe must be to resuscitate the 'Forgotten Agenda' of Maastricht. The first issue is the single market, where tariff and other protectionist measures are dissolved. The process moves to its fulfilment on 31 December 1992. Now that President Mitterand's EC referendum vote is in the bag – just – it should go straight to the central issue of the CAP subsidies and the Uruguay Round of the GATT talks. This will inevitably reopen the debate on the EC itself having to run a balanced budget and reform its burgeoning bureaucracy based in Brussels. These are the immediate tasks that should concern Britain, rather than the distractions of Maastricht or post-Maastricht. There is no point in imposing EMU on a non-common market, nor until the great debate on the proper incidence of taxation has been discussed, argued and settled. Otherwise EMU merely imposes a currency straight-jacket on the fiscal distortions surrounding the confidence trick of protectionist subsidies, especially the CAP.

As is often the case, however, the issue of the hour is not the real issue. Britain can best help herself and the EC by restructuring her own economy in accordance with basic economic principles. Indeed whether Britain can seriously consider joining a federalist economic structure with its own internal structural problems and fiscal distortions or not is in itself a real question. Either way, Britain needs the next recovery in the 1990s to come to terms with some basic issues, whether it is in the ERM or not. Britain does not need to be a member of the ERM in order to reduce inflation. Britain's inflation in 1980-81 peaked at 22% (see Graph 6). Britain was not in the ERM then, but during 1982 inflation fell and by early 1983 was under 4%, achieved by strict adherence to money-supply targets and by letting market forces determine the exchange rate value of the pound. In the two years ended 31 March 1983, sterling fell by 25% against its trade-weighted index, by 27% against the Deutschemark and by 40% against the US dollar. No shade of Creative or Degenerate Person said at the time that this policy was in any way wrong in principle or harmful in effect. There is, moreover, no conclusive argument which says that interest rates should determine exchange rates or vice versa. The ERM fixes the exchange rates and then the theory runs that the unelected bankers at the ECB fix the interest rates for all EC members. In effect, under EMU, the ERM drives each member's macro-economic policies and decisions. This may be good for Germany's authority with its strong Deutschemark and its alliance with France, with their mutual interest in the anti-common market CAP subsidies. It was not good for Britain in 1992, however, when the German recession and costs of reunification were being dumped on its already battered economy by the workings of the ERM.

Britain needs lower real interest rates as soon as possible. This is because there is a clear need to stimulate demand at the same time as stimulating domestic production. With inflation under 3.6% and falling, and with real asset deflation across the economy not included in the official inflation figures, interest rates could come down by at least 4% to 6%. (As I write, they have come down 2% to 8% – bravo!) The prospect that horrifies the Foreign Exchange markets is that with a devalued currency, Britain's recovery will suck in imports. A cheap currency will therefore stoke inflation as imported prices will be that much higher because of sterling's weakness. HM Treasury and the Bank of England therefore advise keeping interest rates up so as to keep sterling's value abroad up as well, regardless of the domestic consequences of high interest rates on industry, jobs and investment. What neither institution apparently sees is that lower interest rates will help industry's recovery, while raising taxation by a new community value tax would stifle inflation by keeping property values in line. This approach would also keep government debt down and check the inevitable, mad consumer boom that would otherwise be unleashed. With this shift in the incidence of taxation, interest rates could fall to 6% even as the Prime Minister told the Tory Party Conference at Brighton why his strategy was to keep them up. He is talking to the Foreign Exchange markets while industry collapses in a heap behind his back, but the foreigners looking at him see the slumped body of John Bull lying on the ground anyway and so they sell sterling lower all the same. The advantages of the approach of lowering interest rates and raising local taxes is that interest is paid to international bankers while tax payments stay in the local economy. Lower interest rates help industry and higher local taxes keep property prices and inflation down. The point is that higher local taxes enable interest rates to come down. Any other combination only creates another problem. There is no alternative. Mr Prime Minister, please wake up!

The pound could and would find its own level outside the ERM, regardless. In fact it might only fall temporarily, as markets took stock of the political certainty of Britain until 1996-97 and the looming uncertainty in Germany, caused by reunification, and the probability of earlier recovery in Britain. She could, and should, announce a strategic switch in emphasis from property to industry, to be brought about by fiscal restructuring, which would boost domestic and international confidence. The real danger is the failure to realise that the setback in property values is a disguised long-term blessing. The heads of two major British banks and several building societies have recently called for 'lower interest rates to bring about a recovery in the housing market'. Their proposals boil down to the Treasury sending a big cheque round – 'motor-bike will do' – to pay for their property loan losses. Their belief is that rising house values will lead to a consumer recovery, as confidence improves. They also overlook the parlous state of manufacturing, and forget that Britain's retailers will simply suck in imports, that sterling will fall further and sow the seeds for the next bout of inflation. Mr Banker, please wake up too!

No! The time has come to bite the bullet on the myth of false property values. They are a deception that has induced property mania. If the value of your house doubles, so has the next house you buy, as well as the one your children will eventually buy. These constantly rising prices simply keep the chain of debt around the nation's neck. They are the main cause of Britain's economic ills. The population has already endured most of the pain. The time has come to switch taxation from industry to property, to the order of £25 billion per annum in 1990 prices, introduced over the rest of the decade, but as swiftly as circumstances allow.

The banks will argue against such a move, as they count the horrendous illiquidity that their own excessive property lending has created. The moral issue is clear enough: they lent out on property values created by the community, to the extent of the site value element. The practical issue is also clear enough: Britain has too many banks and far too many building societies. There are at least ten major British banks. There is only room for about half that number. Lloyds Bank's failed bid for Midland Bank in 1992 was based purely on the pressing rationale for restructuring through mergers. Lloyds

Bank was right and the process is inevitable. Britain has seventy-eight building societies. There is only room for about twenty. In the merger process the weakest banks and building societies will have to sell their capital and reserves for what they are worth, paying in effect for the losses on property loans. These mergers, as regards banks at any rate, will become inevitable under the new banking solvency rules as the accountancy profession belatedly realises it cannot go on signing off balance sheets in the financial services sector indefinitely, indicating assets which have long since lost their 'permanent' value. The government will have to move quickly as interest rates fall to nip the imminent rise in property values in the bud. (Remember how quickly the property boom got going in the 1980s?) It is not even a question of political will. Property markets will never be the same again, not at least in the 45-year downturn in the long cycle, and the banking shake-up is in the air anyway, whatever the government does or does not do. At least the consumer might find a proper bakery and ironmonger reappearing in the High Street, as property values and rents tumble and labour-intensive businesses built on real service begin to thrive again.

How was the amount of the £25 billion shift in taxation arrived at? Local authority expenditure in 1990 was £57.4 billion. Rates (and community charge) funded only £13.9 billion of this amount, with rent and interest income funding another £5.5 billion. The shortfall not funded by local taxes and income was therefore around £38 billion. The education budget in 1990 amounted to £20.4 billion, which will be removed to the central government's budget. The balance in unfunded local expenditure is therefore £17.6 billion. Local taxes will have to raise £31.5 billion by the year 2000 at 1990 prices, which would put them on a quantum level with VAT, which is set to raise £35.7 billion in 1991-92 and £40 billion in 1992-93. Local authorities must also cut profligate expenditure and charge for local services to the extent of a further 10% of their budgets, say approximately £6 billion, so local taxes must rise by £25 billion. There is no rational reason for any objections to such increases, as homeowners are only then paying for what they receive in actual local services, after excluding education. This tax will be assessed on the basis of site values and not developed values, so no property improvement suffers tax. The argument that people will not be able to pay does not stand up either. The increase is the same quantum as the public absorbed in increased VAT between 1980 and 1991. Moreover income tax has been reduced from 1979 to 1988 from 83% to 40% at the higher rate, and to 20%-25% at the lower rate in 1992. This increase in local taxes would amount to only 2.8% of the 1987 valuation of properties set out in Table 2. If the imposition of this tax coincides with interest rate reductions approaching base rates of 6%, and in a maintained anti-inflation environment, property prices will not fall in value below the level they will probably reach in the 1991-93 property downturn anyway. The point is they will stay there and keep inflation down as well. The message is that lower house prices do *not* damage your wealth. They preserve your job.

Chancellors should always look for ways of cutting wasteful or unfair taxation, particularly as the central government rate support grant is now being reduced by £31.5 billion in the 1990s. The car tax is being reduced from £1.3 billion to £700 million in the year to 1992-93. It should be removed altogether. Competitive pressures arising from over-capacity in the industry and the recession will ensure that the full reduction, about £600 in the price of a compact car, will flow through to the consumer. In reducing any taxation on industry it must be considered who will be the ultimate beneficiary, land or labour, as was observed with the [Agricultural De-] Rating Act of 1929. If the reduction is not passed through to the consumer, the landlords of Britain's garages will gradually raise rents as the tenants make more profits, but the new community value tax will now catch this increase for the community. Capital gains tax also raises only £1.4 billion, despite being set at a far higher rate than any other G7 country. It should be scrapped, for one very good reason. People invest from their savings, which have already been taxed once before. It is quite immoral for any government to tax a fund that has been taxed already. The same may be said of inheritance tax too, which only raises £1.3 billion. Why does the government think it can take someone's possessions simply because they are deceased? Most people do not leave their money to the government in their wills. They leave it to their families or to the dogs' home. It is the work of Degenerate Persons who are driven by the politics of envy and think the state has an inherent right to take two bites out of its citizens' apples. In fact the current Conservative government acknowledges the principle that is at stake here, as privately held businesses, including farms, are now exempt from inheritance tax altogether. Why are they exempt and not people's savings? What does the Treasury say to that? The removal of capital gains tax will encourage savings, set the stock market alight, attract inward investment and enable industry to raise capital more easily and on better terms. Why prevent all those good things for the sake of a mere billion pounds of double 'envy' tax? There was no capital gains tax before 1965 and there is no need of one in the future. The removal of inheritance tax will also encourage savings and provide the capital for the next generation to become more self-sufficient or even self-sustaining entrepreneurs. That can only be good too. The political and economic argument for the removal of these two taxes is that the new community value tax will itself tax away gains on property investment and speculation and largely reduce the tax-take from these two taxes anyway.

The introduction of an annual community value tax will reduce property prices. This will be excellent news for first-time house-buyers and businesses. It will be cheaper to buy property. It also means that consumer purchasing power will be gradually increased, giving time to home industries to invest to meet the demand. Stamp duty on property transfers can now be abolished too. The bureaucracy will need less tax advisers and inspectors. They can be retrained for industry and commerce. To help this reallocation of resources, other taxes, which hardly pay their cost of collection, can also be abolished, including petroleum revenue tax, agricultural levies and stamp duty on share transfers. The cost of government is now coming down too, and not a day too soon. What is this expense called 'Other Departments' in the Budget Report anyway, costing £31.5 billion in 1991-92, and scheduled to rise by nearly 10% next year to £34.5 billion? How can the Government call for private sector pay restraint and reduction in its cost base when it is not doing the same with its own finances. This figure needs explanation. There is none in the Budget. The taxpayers (or borrowers) demand to be informed about this increase!

In order to off-set the removal of the car tax, there should be a sharp increase in tax on leaded fuels. Consideration should also be given to raising petrol duties anyway, to discourage unnecessary journeys, single commuting by car, using a larger car when a smaller one is adequate and, not least, encouraging the use of public transport. Britain has more public ground transport than practically any other country and the resources should be used as much as possible, for both ecological and economical reasons. There should also be a system of taxes, or fiscal fines, for pollution offenders of all types. Industrial processes that discharge into rivers and the atmosphere must expect to pay heavy fines on their revenues from such operations. A new carbon tax will be introduced for emissions into the atmosphere of carbon-based gases which cause acid rain and ozone depletion. Now the Department of the Environment can start paying for itself and really help the ecological environment at the same time.

Finally, the soaring level of health costs must be examined. Since the discovery of AIDS a decade ago, over 3,000 Britains have suffered unpleasant and expensive deaths from this disease. There is, however, a drug-induced death that caused 38,552 equally unpleasant and expensive recorded deaths in Britain (excluding Ulster) in 1991 alone. Not only that, but this drug was advertised on billboards! Unlike other drugs, people take this one in public. In crowded places, it is socially and medically offensive. Yes, smoking has definitely damaged the nation's wealth. The duty on cigarettes will therefore be raised by up to 15%, while more accurate data on the age profile of the victims and on the direct and indirect costs to the nation of its only legalised addictive drug, often inhaled into the respiratory system which is designed to capture oxygen, is examined.

Householders facing sharply higher local taxes, to be phased in during the rest of the decade, will be doing their sums. Their cars will be cheaper, or cost their employer less if it is a company car, leaving the individual a bargaining counter in that instance. The reductions in capital gains tax, inheritance tax and stamp duty will be most welcome and will boost confidence, but they hardly help with the increased annual expenditure. Over time, their savings and the income from them will rise. The householder will be listening to this budget for the 1990s, with some apprehension at this time. 'Before I come to the relief to be granted to householders in the transition phase of moving £25 billion in taxation from industry to property...' intones the Chancellor, enticingly, before continuing to remove once and for all the absurd subsidy to private ownership of houses, namely the tax relief on interest on the first £30,000 of mortgage loan. The Budget Report, 1992-93 costs this subsidy for home ownership at £6.1 billion (page 60). It is a straight subsidy to house prices which reflects straight into higher land prices! It will have to go. A homeowner will face a deduction of £1,200 per annum in extra income tax as a result, on the basis of a home loan rate of 10%, to be phased in by the year 2000. This will be off-set, however, by a surprise and immediate reduction in VAT from 17.5% to 15%, costing nearly £6 billion in 1992-93. The immediate cash boost to the consumer will go to an immediate revival in consumer confidence and the recession will ensure that the full reduction is passed on to the consumer.

Before jettisoning the mortgage interest tax relief for good, however, there is a neat possibility for the Chancellor to smooth the introduction of the new community value tax so as to prevent house and other property prices plunging even further. The Chancellor could actually increase the level of mortgage interest tax relief for new buyers. An increase in the qualifying mortgage limit for new mortgages could be paid for by cutting the mortgage interest tax relief on existing mortgages. This switch would stimulate and steady the housing market, as the whole system depends on the first-time buyer entering the market, in order for the rest of the chain to move. The actual amounts and proportions could be adjusted in the light of actual circumstances, particularly interest rates, so that by the end of the decade the mortgage interest tax relief subsidy was completely removed, at no extra cost to the Treasury in the meantime. Now, that is a calculation that the Treasury computer could actually get the right answer on.

Our average homeowner is now fiddling with a calculator in earnest to work out whether he or she is a net gainer or loser. There is an immediate gain on VAT, which has been reduced to the EC's new minimum threshold of 15%. Mortgage tax relief currently of the order of £1,200 per annum is disappearing at around £200 per annum, so there is plenty of time to adjust to that. The problem is the increase in rates or local taxes coming in over the same period by the introduction of community value tax and how to pay for it. This will keep property values down, as deliberate policy! What will happen to over-borrowed homeowners, caught in the mortgage trap? The key will lie mainly in interest rates, which will come down in the worldwide recovery, and quickly too now that Britain is out of the ERM. No one knows for certain when that will be, but each day that the recession continues brings recovery one day nearer, and the switch in the incidence of taxation is being phased in over five to seven years. This process will be accelerated as recovery gathers strength and in any event as soon as property prices start moving upwards at a rate quicker than inflation. This inflation will be positively pounced on by a graded increase in community value tax.

But there is another key to open the mortgage trap with. If someone is living in a £50,000 house that has a £75,000 mortgage, does it matter if they move to a £60,000 house with an £85,000 mortgage? Of course it doesn't, provided that their income has gone up. If their income has not gone up in real terms, does it matter if they take a £15,000 loss and buy another house at the same price in the depressed market? Of course it doesn't! In fact high house-prices are actually a myth. If your house shoots up in value, so too has the next house you will one day buy, and vice versa. It is better to destroy the myth than the whole economy, for heaven's sake! The estate agents can now handle another product, the 'transferable, insured mortgage', or TIM. To keep TIM company, we can also promote TESS', whereby the mortgage company ' takes equity share/securitisation', cancelling debt in exchange for a percentage of ownership. In effect the market will force acceptance of the reality that the debt is secured on individuals' earnings and not on the property. The good news for Joe and Jane Six-Pack is that they can move house and still afford the beer. All these insurance companies that lost several billion pounds propping up the boom prices could now make it all back again by insuring the repayments of the losses from their past errors.

The Chancellor meanwhile has £31.5 billion savings in his sight over the medium term from increased local taxes and income charges, plus cost reductions. There is a recovery of over £6 billion on mortgage interest relief that has already been given away in a VAT reduction in 1993-94. As the aim is to prevent property prices and inflation rising, the trick will be to implement these plans as quickly as recovery allows. To balance the books, the Chancellor should cut central rate support grant by at least £6-£8 billion in 1993-94. That will make room for up to £2-£3 billion in cash to stimulate industrial investment, in 1993-94, as the first stage of a more general recovery in 1994-95. At this point, the Chancellor's sums appear as on Table 8.

Table 8: Proposed Budget Changes, 1993-94
£0,000,000,000 (billions)

	–	+
VAT reduction from 17.5% to 15%	6.0	–
Rate support grant reduction	–	8.0
Mortgage interest relief cancellation	–	1.0
Industrial investment incentives (accelerated investment allowances/grants etc)	2.0	–
Increases in tobacco duties	–	1.0
Abolition of redundant taxes on production:		
* Petroleum revenue tax	–*	–
* Capital gains tax	1.4	–
* Car tax	1.3	–
* Agricultural levies	–*	–
Abolition of other taxes:		
* Inheritance tax	1.3	–
* Stamp duties	2.1	–
New Green Taxes:		
* Green tax on leaded fuels	–	2.0
* Carbon and pollution tax	–	2.1
	£14.1 Bn	£14.1Bn

* less than £500 million

Note: any shortfall will add to the PSBR in the short term.

The Chancellor and employers have to take care over the mortgage interest tax phase-out. This removal of a tax subsidy will hit taxpayers with mortgages up to £30,000. They will pay more tax as this subsidy is progressively withdrawn. However, the earlier analysis of income tax as a payroll tax showed that the tax is paid for and borne by the employer, not the employee. As more income tax becomes payable with the removal of the subsidy, the employer is paying over more income tax. It becomes essential that employers hold gross wages in real terms. Otherwise the removal of the subsidy will turn itself into an added charge to employers' profit and loss accounts. Hence the strategy of immediately reducing VAT by the same quantum amount, so that the employers are forearmed to make the tax increase stick on employees' property and not on their employment by the employer.

In 1994-95 an investment-led recovery is beginning and interest rates have fallen to 6%. Interest rates will stay lower as Britain is at last taxing one of the twin spirals of inflation, namely surging property prices. The removal of the mortgage interest tax relief is quickly catching up the VAT reduction, which helped spur consumer confidence. Reductions in central rate support grant and the consequent increase in local community value tax are keeping ahead of interest rate reductions – a delicate exercise. The Chancellor is now able to plan for where the rest of the £25 billion saving on local rates support grant will be utilised in the medium and longer term in reducing other taxation. There is an obvious target: the employer's share of social security, formerly national insurance, which cost industry £20 billion in 1990. Over the decade it will simply be eliminated, progressively. There is a boost to business confidence and employment of enormous proportions from this initiative. Investment from America, Japan and the EC will flow into the UK, bringing know-how and management skills. Unemployment will tumble, and as it tumbles so does government expenditure on unemployment and the PSBR. This is inevitable as the social security payments are a tax on employment. Their removal lowers the cost of employment. The lower the cost of anything in the capitalist marketplace, the greater the demand for it, and employment is just another commodity and no exception. The aim should be to halve unemployment to under 1.5 million and produce an annual saving of at least £15 billion by the year 2000 in the social security budget. The fall in the PSBR is most welcome too, as the Government's interest bill for 1991-92 is estimated at £15.4 billion and local authorities' interest bill at £5.6 billion. This cool £21 billion cash outflow for being in debt represents 4.4% of 1990's GDP of £477.7 billion. One of the reasons taxation must be moved on to properties is that this debt has now got to be reduced in the downturn of the long cycle – both private sector debt and national debt. After the next dip in the short cycle, debt will turn into a killer. Every £1 repaid before the year 2000 will be worth £2 or more thereafter, as the ability to repay from earnings or GDP dries up as the long downturn takes hold.

The £20 billion progressive cancellation of employers' social security contributions will be the biggest opportunity since WW2 for industry to invest in equipment, training, research and development, marketing and new product launches. It will bring employment unit costs down and make Britain a key economy for foreign manufacturing transplants and implants for companies targeting the 320 million consumers already in the EC. By reducing the cost of employment, unemployment is bound to reduce. What is the cost of unemployment in fact? The 1991-92 budget for social security is £58.3 billion (see Table 2), but the Budget Report 1992-93 gives no analysis. It merely states (page 62) that for '1993-94 the planning total was increased by £13 billion. The new plans reflect the unavoidable pressures of the economic cycle, especially on social security...' In other words, the recession that the Treasury did not see coming, exacerbated by the Treasury's ill-considered boost to the economy in 1988, has meant unemployment rising way beyond the Treasury's more recent predictions, which even now are not properly disclosed. The report also states (page 68) that 'the latest forecast of general government receipts for [social security] for 1991-92 is £3.25 billion lower... reflecting the downward revision to the forecast of economic activity in the second half of 1991'. So 1991-92 forecast receipts are going down and 1992-93 expenses are going up, but how much of social security relates to unemployment benefit? The latest *Blue Book* for 1991 shows 1990s unemployment benefit at only £780 million, having peaked in 1986 at £1.8 billion. The total budget for social security funds in 1990 was £36.4 billion, compared with the 1991-92 latest budget forecast of £61.5 billion, rising in 1992-93 to £66 billion. The scale of these increases is breathtaking.

There is a sneaking suspicion that the actual debt Britain is planning to take on in 1992-93, namely the PSBR of £28.1 billion, is wholly to pay for the cost of unemployment in the recession. If individuals went to see their bank manager to borrow money so that they could put their feet up for a year and not work, we all know what the answer would be. The fact that a nation borrows to pay for around 3,000,000 of its inhabitants to do exactly that is no less crazy. Just like the individual, the nation takes on a debt because it has not got its own money. The debt and the interest on it will have to be repaid from future earnings. The cause of unemployment has already been tracked down to inflation. Inflation is caused by pay awards running ahead of productivity, which immediately reflect in a rise in land values, or in community value that is left in the owners' hands. By not taxing that value, the nation has to borrow instead, which becomes another cost that inevitably falls mainly on industry.

With due deference to Keynes, it would seem more sensible at least to try and get some value back from this vast and economically pointless 'investment' in enforced idleness. The Department of Trade and Industry (DTI) spent millions of pounds recently proclaiming in expensive TV advertisements that it was infused with the 'Enterprise Initiative'. Every major High Street in Britain has a Jobcentre. The Jobcentres unfortunately do not have any jobs. There are public buildings, such as town halls, libraries, hospitals, schools, swimming pools, museums, fire stations, police stations, railway stations, law courts, prisons, bus shelters, recycling centres and many more, crying out for running repairs, repainting and renovations. There are thousands of former executives and 250,000 construction workers out of work. Hand tools, paint, wood and other materials only cost a fraction of a worker's pay. Surely, the DTI can work with the Department of Employment to mobilise the existing and available resources to obtain some economic return from all this wastage. The armed forces know only too well how inactivity leads to demoralisation and long-term idleness. Unemployment has the same negative psychological effects too. The armed forces overcome this by giving the idle pair of hands a paint pot and a brush, with the order: 'If it stands still, paint it! If it moves, salute it!' The Jobcentres could be full of temporary work. The unemployed who hate the idleness would be hard at it, for which they should receive a financial incentive above the dole payment. And employers in the recovery would ask new employees if they had availed themselves of the DTI's 'Enterprise Work Scheme'.

I only mention this in outline and by way of digression because, under Britain's existing fiscal structure, unemployment in the new millennium may reach unheard of levels and be the source of civil disturbance. Besides, any group of high-ranking Degenerate Persons who plan to borrow £13.8 billion in 1991-92 followed by £28.1 billion in 1992-93 and probably over £40 billion in 1993-94 with nothing to show for it, should not themselves be in that office, for the nation cannot afford it. Bearing in mind the economic long cycle, the decade of the 1990s is the time to repay debt, not increase it. If Britain has to borrow at the height of the economic cycle to fund social security, the Welfare State will become the Farewell State in the long downturn. The economy cannot pay for its present level of unemployment 'benefits'. ('Benefits' are in inverted commas as there are no benefits from unemployment, only financial and human costs.) Now there is talk of cancelling the new underground to Canary Wharf in Docklands. Why not build it and create employment and a long-term asset and have something to show for the borrowing? It would be a strategic investment and force rents lower throughout the South-East, helping the fight against inflation as a result.

The arguments for pressing on with the Jubilee Line are overwhelming from a fiscal point of view. London Underground commissioned a report from Professor Douglas McWilliams who asserts that 46% to 47% of the government's costs would be recovered during the period of construction in tax revenues and saved public expenditure on unemployment and other social security costs of the 12,000 workforce required for the project. What the good professor, HM Treasury, the administrators, the construction companies, the banks and the government have failed to spot is that the whole project is probably self-financing anyway in view of the increased land values that will be created from Green Park to Stratford in East London, where the line will link to Eurotunnel's terminal. Just think of the annual land value that the new community value tax will catch and the project is funded before you can blink. The only possible losers would be White's, who will suffer the indignity of finding themselves on top of one of the busiest underground stations in the capital. That should add extra piquancy to their 'shit of the year' award. It might even go to HM Treasury, if it ever woke up to the opportunity staring it in the face!

In fact the introduction of the community value tax is the key that the Keynesians lack to unlock the funding capability of other valuable infrastructure projects, such as the electrification of the railway line linking London with the Eurotunnel terminal in Kent which requires £1 billion. There is a world of difference between a PSBR taken on to pay unemployment 'benefit', which yields no return and is irrecoverable, and borrowings taken on for a valuable project that generates future revenue. The *Red Book*'s PSBR requirement should set out the latter clearly, so that foreign investors can see what they are funding. With community value tax in place, however, a whole realm of infrastructure projects become viable as a major engine of economic recovery. And the funding now falls on local government. Quite simply, the boroughs that will benefit from the community value could form a consortium to borrow the funds against the project on their own.

The minor digression on the small matter of an unexplained requirement to borrow £28.1 billion in 1992-93 has left our nervous homeowner wondering about the outcome of the 1990s budget plan. The Chancellor has announced the intention of reducing mortgage interest rate tax relief as interest rates decline. Also, the central government rate support grant will be progressively reduced by £31.5 billion, so that local rates on both business premises and residences rise to around £40 billion in real terms, allowing for income increases and cost decreases. Based on the 1987 property valuations set out in Table 3, the level of former local rates would have had to amount to a shade over 4% of property values, so that a £250,000 house would bear old-style rates of about £10,000. Under the proposal to levy local taxes on site value only, the actual sum payable will be less on properties located on smaller sites and will be more on properties on more central or larger sites, whether they be business or residential premises, which can only be fair and probably very much in line with the ability to pay. In practice ratepayers really will take much more interest in what their local authorities are now spending their money on. Judging by some of the items set out in the *UK National Accounts, 1991*, there should be plenty of savings to be had. For instance, nearly £2.2 billion on 'recreational and cultural affairs', £567 million on 'community development', over £5 billion on 'personal social services' and £423 million 'concessionary fares' could usefully by put under the electorate's spotlight. Similarly, income from housing, amenities and services will have to be maximised and loss-making ventures curtailed. What is certain is that local authorities are going to be accountable for every penny, and not a day too soon. I suspect that savings approaching 15% or more are attainable. As my secretary typed this section of the manuscript, she informed me that her local authority, the Labour-controlled Greenwich Council, runs a 'lesbian crèche', whatever that is! The Treasury should send a grammarian immediately to sort out this queer oxymoron.

Back to serious matters: how is the householder going to pay for the sharp increase in local authority taxation? There will naturally be the usual arrangements to reduce the tax for old age pensioners, students and other special cases. First, existing householders in employment have already benefitted from the massive reductions in income tax in the 1980s, and they will clearly have to allocate part of these savings to pay for their own local taxes, which pay nothing other than their local services. New homeowners and tenants will benefit from much lower house prices and rents than pertained in the 1980s, so their outgoings on mortgage repayments and rent will be much reduced. Like the residential tenant, businesses will benefit from static rents on existing leases and lower rents on new leases, as local taxes directly reduce rent. It will do this by forcing landlords to put property on the market at any price they can get, as they have to pay the full community value tax. In addition, legislation will be passed outlawing 'upward only' rent review provisions. In the new anti-inflationary environment, these inflation-inducing terms cannot be tolerated. There will clearly be painful adjustments for many. Some will have to sell up and buy smaller premises. Others will have to sell or rent out the second home. Others will have to take on overtime or evening work in the reviving economy, or the marital partner will have to generate some income. Some will have to ask grown up children in employment and living at home to contribute. There is nothing unfair or unreasonable in this. Repayment of the excessive debt taken on in the 1980s is bound to be painful. Householders are only paying for the police protection, rubbish removal, fire service, street lighting and other services that are located in their own community and their share is fixed by the site value of the property they enjoy. The idea that industry can somehow continue paying their bills and compete in the world at the same time is a fiction. The natural laws, like markets, simply cannot be bucked any longer. The fourth principle of economics stated that what is given freely by the earth, in this case the community site value, is for distribution to meet the community's needs.

The homeowner is also nervous about repossession of his home by the building society or bank lender. Even before the hefty and healthy increases in local taxes, there are 330,000 mortgagors in arrears and over a million householders in the so-called mortgage trap, where the value of the house is less than the outstanding debt and where the building societies and insurance companies have not yet thought through the solutions. In the earlier discussion on the interaction of land and labour it was seen how losses on property lending were written off for tax purposes and that the Treasury paid in effect for the first 35% of property losses. It was also seen how the level of property lending was itself inflationary. Consequently the Chancellor will now announce that, as from the beginning of the tax year 1993-94, any bad loan secured on or advanced for the purpose of property purchase will not be an allowable deduction for tax purposes. In effect the lender takes all the loss.

This fiscal change will immediately put an end to excessive property loans, which even went as high as 100% of the cost in the 1980s. Lenders will now have to obey the rules of normal prudence. Any loan over 67% of a property could only be contemplated to a really sound borrower. A level of 50% will be nearer the market average. These practices will dampen credit-driven booms, keep property prices low and taxes higher. The lenders will argue that this proposed change is retrospective tax legislation and should not apply to existing loans. This argument is false. In preparing their annual accounts up to 31 December in any one year banks and other lenders are required to make specific provisions (as apposed to general provisions) for bad and doubtful debts so as to present a 'true and fair view'. Such provisions at 31 December 1992 will be calculated on the bottom of the market. These preliminary results are announced at the end of February 1993 and signed off by the auditors at the end of March 1993. They can hardly complain that they should not be able to make further provisions against their existing loan book in the future. Otherwise they are saying their 1992 accounts are not 'true and fair'. Having closed the tax book on the excesses of past lending, every time a lender forces repossession in the future, they will now take the first 35% loss instead of the Treasury, or rather industry. For the year 1992, however, an additional once-off tax relief will be necessary to grant a tax write-off on general provisions which are not normally allowable. This is good news for struggling borrowers. The lenders have a strong interest in sitting it out with them and will have to listen attentively to any proposals that borrowers make to alter the terms of the original loan, like converting it to a new transferable, insured mortgage, or TIM for the ad-persons. Alternatively the lender could take an equity stake/securitisation, or TESS'. There is no room for sympathy with the banks and building societies. They went in with their eyes open, or possibly shut, and in either case have no one to blame but themselves and their own profligacy. Nor can banks and building societies go on a 'loan strike'. Their overheads are too high and their outlets too numerous by far, so that they cannot afford to become underlent. In fact there is likely to be more volume at the lower overall level of advance, which will help the market get moving. It is only stuck, after all, because the average level of advance is too high in the first place. In fact this fiscal alteration will rapidly be perceived as beneficial for the long-term health of the lending institutions as well. At the same time, debt on HLTs which are declared to be hostile takeovers by the Monopolies and Mergers Commission and/or Takeover Panel will be similarly disallowed for tax in the event of loss.

This change in the taxation rules for bad property loans and hostile HLTs will save something over a billion pounds a year for the next three years at least, in the form of increased corporation tax receipts. These funds will be used to launch a new initiative in industrial training schemes, as approved by the DTI, or private organisations with enterprise and initiative. While the recession continues, the Treasury will advance half or more of the costs of approved new training and retraining schemes, with companies undertaking to pay the balance, on the basis that they continue with their level of expenditure to the year 2000, in fact right through the next recovery. Permanent fiscal incentives for companies for training programmes will be put in place during the recovery.

New employment prospects are more likely to be generated by SMEs than by big business. The European Commission has defined an SME as any firm with a workforce of not more than 500 workers and net fixed assets of not more than ECU 75 million, and not more than a third of its capital held by a larger company. SMEs account for over 95% of EC companies and for approximately two-thirds of total EC employment. During the 1980s, the pension funds raised their 'alternative asset' allocation for development capital up to 2% – 5% of gross assets in Britain, and even up to 15% in some cases in America. These institutions, quite rightly, are investing for their pensioners and shareholders' profits and not for any altruistic reasons. The exceptional institution was 3i (Investors in Industry), capitalised in 1946 by the big banks to provide capital for reconstruction and with a long-term investment strategy. Unfortunately the banks typically need to cash in their profit on these industrial investments to pay for property losses, so 3i will be floated in the near future and this will probably affect its investment criteria, bringing in shorter time horizons for investments. The institutions will continue to invest in the sector, but more early-stage/higher-risk capital is still needed. Mrs Thatcher's government introduced the Business Expansion Scheme (BES) in the mid-1980s, whereby individuals could invest up to £40,000 in each tax year in a new business venture, and write off the investment against tax payable, provided it was held for five years, when any gain would not be subject to capital gains tax. (Note the precedent.)

It would make far more commercial sense to give a boost to corporate venturing, introducing a Corporate BES, so that companies could invest and save tax. It matters not to HM Treasury whether it gives an effective tax-break to GEC or to 'Sid', as it is only money. A Corporate BES will be introduced, so that companies can invest 5% of their tax payments (not taxable profits) into qualified funds. These funds must be managed by approved members of the British Venture Capital Association and only invest in companies whose activities would be dealt with under the 'Manufacturing' sector of the UK National Accounts, as defined. Investments must be held for five years, and anyway capital gains tax will have already been abolished. In one sense it is a sad reflection on the lack of appetite in the UK for corporate venturing to need a fiscal incentive. On the Continent corporate venturing develops new technologies and processes, but in the UK it generally falls to the finance director to run the programme. It needs a fiscal rationale to stimulate risk investment for the future. Nevertheless the cost to the Treasury will not be 5% of total corporation tax, as many companies will still pay tax and ignore the opportunity. The scheme would probably cost about £500 million per annum, which is about 0.1% of GDP.

That is not much of an investment in future manufacturing. More will have to be done. The system of capital investment allowances in manufacturing, construction and transport equipment and associated support hardware will be adjusted to provide a 100% allowance on the date of investment. In effect HM Treasury will 'pay' for the re-equipment of British industry, in respect of profitable and therefore tax-paying companies. The scheme will not pay for non-manufacturing industries. If a building society buys a new computer system it would not qualify. Only the 'manufacturing' and 'construction' sectors of the economy would qualify. The annual cost can be estimated from historic data when 'first-year allowances' existed, but I have assumed the cost to be around £2.0 billion per annum. It could well be higher, and the higher the better.

This budget for the 1990s was aimed at switching the incidence of taxation from industry on to property, with consequent reductions in unemployment, with funding local government expenditure by revenue from local taxes, by removing the boom-bust cycle in property values and the economy and with curbing property lending and property-induced inflation. The result is set out in Table 9.

Income tax has risen by £6.1 billion as a result of the complete phasing out of mortgage interest relief, which was a direct subsidy to house prices, or more specifically to site values. Corporation tax has gained about £1 billion from phasing out the deductibility of bad loans on property acquisitions. The investment incentives on industrial investment and the corporate BES proposals have been assumed to cost £3 billion. VAT has been reduced by the reduction from 17.5% to 15%. Petrol duties on leaded fuels have been increased by £1.5 billion, and tobacco duties on cigarettes are up £1 billion to pay for the resultant health care costs. Social security receipts are down £20 billion by cancellation of the employers' liability, and the employees' liability will be renamed and become the next target for elimination. Community value tax is set to raise nearly £35 billion. It is shown in parentheses as it will not appear on the central government's budget, as it will be levied and collected by local government. On the expenses side of the budget, rate support grant of £52.5 billion disappears and not a day too soon. Education returns to central government at a cost of just over £20 billion. A saving of £25 billion is assumed in unemployment benefit and other welfare items, as unemployment falls during the decade by over 2,000,000 as the benefits of the new focus on industry, inward investment and the export opportunities, especially in the expanding EC, are seized rather than wasted. Finally, a saving in interest of £4.8 billion is assumed from interest rate reductions and debt repayment.

Table 9: Comparison of 1991-92 Actual Budget with Target for 2000-01
£0,000,000,000s (billions) – 1991-92 prices

Receipts	1991-92	2000-01
Income Tax	59.6	65.7
Corporation Tax	19.5	17.5
Value Added Tax	35.7	29.7
Petrol, Derv. Duties	10.9	12.4
Tobacco Duties	6.1	7.1
Alcohol Duties	5.2	5.2
Vehicle Duties	3.0	3.0
Social Security Receipts	36.7	16.7
Other Income	21.5	21.5
Redundant Taxes (Table 8)	6.3	N/A
	204.5	178.8
Rates*/Community Charge	22.0	N/A
[Community Value Tax	N/A	34.4]
	226.5	[213.2]

* National non-domestic rates and local authority rates

Expenses	1991-92	2000-01
Social Security	58.3	33.3
Health (and OPCS)	24.9	24.9
Defence	22.8	22.8
Provinces	14.7	14.7
Other Departments	31.5	31.5
Rate Support Grant	52.5	N/A
Education	N/A	20.4
Other Items	0.3	0.3
	205.0	147.9
Central Government Debt		
Interest and other adjustments	29.8	25.0
	234.8	172.9
Borrowing (Requirement)/Repayment	(8.3)	5.9
	226.5	178.8

Source: 1991-92 figures from Table 2

The structure of Britain's taxation and of its local government funding is now a replication of the continental European models. The level of British property prices was a myth, but the level of debt was an inflation-inducing reality. The myth has been exploded and the debt bubble should never reappear. Everyone can breathe a sigh of relief, at least for the future. There are only two obstructions, other than HM Treasury, that can get in the way: the 'something for nothing' corrupt attitude which demands that someone else pays the cost of local government – but there is no 'someone else'; and the shortsightedness of the politicians who want to appear to be giving 'something for nothing' to get more votes. The people get the government they deserve. The people need to decide what they want, either prosperity from real earnings in industry or inevitable decline in over-valued and over-borrowed houses. Quite simply, where does the British nation want to be in the spectrum of Creative and Degenerate Person?

It is said that the first step a fleeing person takes from a burning house determines the direction of escape. Britain's economic madhouse is well and truly alight, but running off to join EMU will not put the fire out. It is only the switch in the incidence of taxation back on to property and off industry that can dowse the flames. When a house burns down completely, the only thing that is left is the site itself, which still has its value. The house came from the earth and returns to it in accordance with the first principle of economics. That the site value still remains available for the community is another fundamental principle, as is its corollary, that those who fail to observe the earth's own laws must pay the fitting penalty. Britain has paid dearly for the failure to observe these fundamental principles. The choice is in ourselves to be thus or thus, advised the Bard. Or do we want to dodge the issue and then, like John of Gaunt in his dying speech, proclaim:

That England, that was wont to conquer others,
Hath made a shameful conquest of itself.

The Bard knew what he was stating in this speech from *King Richard the Second*, Act Two, Scene 1. He was warning the nation about the economic dangers inherent in a system of total land privatisation, where the community value was not returned to its source in accordance with the earth's natural laws.

12

Political Postscript

Economic policy is enacted by politicians, who look to professional economists for advice and guidance. Once in power, the burdens of office do not allow time for fundamental research, which seems a very good reason why experienced persons should enter public office; otherwise there is likely to be a policy vacuum, as at present. Unfortunately since WW2 the issue of taxation of community site values and industrial production has not formed any part of mainstream economic thought or debate in the Anglo-American economies. In the second half of the nineteenth century it was the main economic debate on both sides of the Atlantic. In the first decade of the twentieth century it was the burning issue in Britain. It was on the landslide victory of the Liberals (nothing whatever to do with the current Liberals or Liberal-Democrats) – in 1906 that the issue became central to government policy, first under Sir Henry Campbell-Bannerman and then under Herbert Asquith. The 1909 budget sought to shift the incidence of taxation on to site values and property development gains, but was rejected by the House of Lords. It was this rejection of a fiscal measure that led directly to the abrogation of their Lordships' power over the nation's finances enshrined in the Parliament Act. The damage was unfortunately done and WW1, the Great Depression and WW2 switched the emphasis in economic debate and policy to the welfare state and nationalisation of key industries.

The Liberal-Democrats are but a spent force compared to the Liberal Party before and after 1900. The Labour Party that rose from the wreckage of the Liberal feuding has become the political wing of the trade union movement. As such, it concentrates on labour, has forgotten the land issue and usually had problems with money when it was in power. Its electoral promises to the trade unions meant it spent too much, so it had to tax too much and then had to borrow too much, so that inflation rose too much. Then the grey-suited executives of the IMF arrived in London to start balancing the books. Of its two major economic initiatives, the National Health Service has become the most important civilian institution in the country, while nationalisation set British industry back several decades, with low incentive levels, low productivity, poor quality and lousy service. In fact the nationalised industries became mollycoddled monopolies, often run by the trade union demagogues for the grateful workers over the heads of inept management, with customers left waiting and wondering. The result of the very first nationalisation, that of the Bank of England in 1945, has enabled the politicians to mismanage the economy by giving them control over interest rates in every short cycle since WW2. Interest rates have been driven by political and not by monetary considerations.

The Conservative Party of the 1990s is quite different from the party that resisted site value rating and taxation based on land values at the turn of the century. It is also quite different in character and outlook even from the party of the 1960s. Mrs Thatcher changed the character of the party irrevocably between 1979 and 1990, and for the better. Under her direction the Conservative Party took up more of the middle ground and became the party of popular capitalism and entrepreneurialism. Meritocracy was encouraged to the extent that Mr Major could announce, on becoming Prime Minister in 1990, that he wanted to build a 'classless society', an unfortunate phrase in one respect, but we all knew what he meant as he came from good but humble origins. Any Conservative leader who had uttered that phrase before 1964 would have been out on his ear! The Conservative Party now poses as representative of all classes and as the guardian of the nation's best interests. It no longer represents the privileged any more than the poor, the landowner any more than the worker. It is committed to making the economy work, to defeating inflation, to reviving manufacturing – well, the last time they mentioned it, that is what we thought they said! – to reducing unemployment, to balancing the budget and reducing the national debt. It cannot therefore avoid serious consideration of the issues raised in this book, which are not new ideas, but simply historical concepts placed in today's context. (You see, there is a point in studying economics, or even history, after all!)

The Conservative Party's principal economic objective is to defeat inflation, but the untaxed value of land is arguably its primary cause. The Conservatives are against subsidies of any kind, but the biggest subsidy in the economy is the central grant to local authorities. The Conservatives expect people to pay for services they receive, but domestic householders pay for only a fraction of the services they enjoy. The Conservatives are in favour of industrial investment organised by the private sector, but the current level of taxation on industry is debilitating. The Conservatives want the local electorate to make local councils more accountable, but local elections only poll about a third of the electorate. The Conservatives aim to reduce unemployment, but payroll taxes and unnecessarily unfair business rates destroy employment. The Conservatives want a property-owning democracy, but the current level of home repossessions in 1991-92 and the lack of buyers is because prices are out-of-reach. The new community value tax will positively equalise these imbalances. The Conservative Party should adopt it as a key policy. There is no substitute. There are alternatives, but they have not worked as they do not deal with economic reality.

In fact it is not actually true to say that 'the Conservative Party resisted site value rating and taxation based on land values'. As early as 1885 Lord Salisbury, the new Conservative Prime Minister, managed to pass the Irish Land Purchase Act into law, with large support from the Liberals. This act was introduced to enable local farmers to purchase land from their often absent owners with payment spread over forty-nine years. (This was the same passage of time, incidentally, as Torah law stipulated as the time-span for leases in Leviticus, chapter 25, verses 8 to 13). The issue of site value rating came to the forefront of political debate in the autumn of 1897. (The Conservatives were in power from 1895 to 1905.) The London County Council had appointed a committee to liaise with the Conservative government on the issue in 1894. This initiative was followed by Dundee in 1895 and by Glasgow in 1896; and by 1897 over 130 local authorities and assessment agencies in England and 63 in Scotland favoured devolution of powers from Westminster to introduce site value rating. In 1901 a Royal Commission on site value rating concluded that such taxation 'should go in relief of local, not Imperial, taxation'. The Chairman of the Commission, Lord Balfour of Burleigh, the Secretary of State for Scotland and a member of the Conservative Cabinet, signed in favour of this tentative conclusion. In 1902 the Liberals introduced a bill in the House of Commons for site value rating, which was defeated by 71 votes at the second reading. A similar bill was introduced in 1903 and received support from 13 Conservatives and only failed at the second reading by 13 votes. In 1904 another bill passed its second reading in the Conservative-dominated House, receiving support from 33 Ministerialists. In 1905 a similar bill was finally carried by a majority of 90. In 1904 and 1905 the Conservative Whip was actually withdrawn, as it was clear that the party was moving to embrace the concept of site value rating, proposals which were endorsed by Conservative-controlled councils like Liverpool and Croydon. This bill and a similar Scottish bill did not proceed to their later parliamentary stages, although by 1906 518 local authorities had petitioned the Chancellor to introduce site value rating, as parliament was dissolved for a general election.

When the Liberals returned to power in 1906, their efforts to levy taxation based on community land values were focused somewhat surprisingly on Scotland. The proposal for a pilot scheme quickly passed in the Commons but the Lords rejected it in 1907 and maintained blocking tactics on a successor bill throughout 1908. Winston Churchill, a rising member of the government, declared in 1907 that land reform was the most important and certainly the most fundamental part of constructive Liberal social policy. In 1906, 400 MPs petitioned Prime Minister Campbell-Bannerman, and in 1908 250 MPs signed a memorial to Prime Minister Asquith to introduce taxation based on community land values. The 1909 budget sought to raise only £500,000 from such taxes, compared to increases in estate duty of £2,850,000, in income tax of £3,500,000, in liquor licences of £2,600,000 and in tobacco and spirit duties of £3,400,000. (Note the size of these figures in relation to the current budget in Table 2 as an indication of mainly post-WW2 inflation). Unfortunately the debate polarised into a fight by the Liberals to curb the fiscal veto of the House of Lords, which they won, and yielded an opportunity for the Conservatives to defeat the Liberals, which they almost did. It is interesting to note that the Conservatives also wanted to protect home industry with tariffs – an approach directly counter to Conservative policy ever since WW2. The confrontation between the Commons and the Lords led to two general elections in 1910, fought over 'The People's Budget'.

The taxation debate was over-shadowed by the fight with the House of Lords. The Unionists, including Austen Chamberlain, George Wyndham, F.E. Smith and Bonar Law, concluded that taxation based on 'site values must be on the lines of a reform of rating, not as in the [1909] Budget by a new national tax'. The new Conservative and Unionist Party (still going strong today) focused on this key issue at its very inception, as a result of the Unionists' perception. The key issue was that any taxation based on land values was a local taxation and nothing to do with Westminster. In 1913 an influential body of Unionists, including Stanley Baldwin, wrote to the new party leader Bonar Law that 'an attempt to ignore the land problem cannot in the nature of things meet with success... The Ordinary Member or Candidate [will be forced] to expound his views on this topic.'

Alas, the outbreak of WW1 truncated the debate and changed the outline and alliances of each political party. The debate rumbled on between WW1 and WW2, particularly when Viscount Snowden as Chancellor attempted on several occasions to introduce land valuation bills. The Great Depression, however, enabled Neville Chamberlain, the Conservative Chancellor in the new government of 1931 and an ardent anti-land taxer, to throttle the debate until WW2 broke out. It was ironic, by way of an historical footnote, that when the House of Commons shouted at Chamberlain 'Go, for God's sake! Go!' in 1940, Andrew MacLaren, a fervent land taxer from the strident Glasgow school of 'single taxers', rose from the Labour benches and accompanied him from the chamber. MacLaren himself was a conscientious objector in WW1 and sympathised with Chamberlain's humanitarianism, even if he disagreed with his economics. MacLaren knew that Chamberlain was terminally ill. He also knew that WW2 had brought the debate on taxation of land values to an abrupt end. Churchill replaced Chamberlain, and it is fitting that his powerful advocacy of land taxation in 1909-10 should serve as an epilogue to this history (see Insert 6).

Insert 6

'The People's Budget'
- 1909 -

'You are, no doubt, generally acquainted with [the budget proposals]. There is the increase in the income tax of twopence, the further discrimination between earned and unearned income, and the super-tax of sixpence on incomes of over £5,000 a year. There are the increases in estate duties and in the legacy duties, and there are the new duties on stamps; there is the tax on motor cars and petrol, the proceeds of which are to go to the improvement of the roads and the abatement of the dust nuisance; there are the taxes on working class indulgences – namely, the increase in the tax on tobacco and on whisky, which enable the working man to pay his share, as indeed he has shown himself very ready to do; there are the taxes on liquor licences, which are designed to secure for the State a certain special proportion of the monopoly value created wholly by the State and with which it should never have parted; and, lastly, there are the three taxes upon the unearned increment in land, upon undeveloped land, upon the unearned increment in the reversion of leases, and then there is the tax upon mining royalties.

'Now these are the actual proposals of the Budget, and I do not think that, if I had the time, I should find any great difficulty in showing you that there are many good arguments, a great volume of sound reason, which can be adduced in support of every one of these proposals. Certainly there is no difficulty in showing that since the Budget has been introduced there has been no shock to credit, there has been no dislocation of business, there has been no set-back in the beginning of that trade revival about the approach of which I spoke at the beginning of the year, and which is now actually in progress. The taxes which have been proposed have not laid any burden upon the necessaries of life like bread or meat, nor have they laid any increased burden upon comforts like tea and sugar. There is nothing in these taxes which makes it harder for a labouring man to keep up his strength or for the small man of the middle class to maintain his style of living. There is nothing in these taxes which makes it more difficult for any hard-working person, whether he works with his hands or his head, to keep a home together in decent comfort. No impediment has been placed by these taxes upon enterprise; no hampering restrictions interrupt the flow of commerce. On the contrary, if the tax upon spirits should result in a diminution in the consumption of strong drink, depend upon it, the State will gain, and all classes will gain. The health of millions of people, the happiness of hundreds of thousands of homes, will be sensibly improved, and money that would have been spent upon whisky will flow into other channels, much less likely to produce evil and much more likely to produce employment. And if the tax on undeveloped land, on land, that is to say, which is kept out of the market, which is held up idly in order that its owner may reap unearned profit by the exertions and through the needs of the surrounding community, if that tax should have the effect of breaking this monopoly and of making land cheaper, a tremendous check on every form of productive activity will have been removed. All sorts of enterprises will become economically possible which are now impossible owing to the artificially high prices of land, and new forces will be liberated to stimulate the wealth of the nation.'

Mr Winston S. Churchill, Liberal MP for Oldham, speaking in Lancashire, December, 1909.

13

Ecological Postscript

The Creator in his wisdom put the human race, animals, trees and plants on the surface of the earth's body, so that they might lead their lives in pure air and support each other in the natural life-force cycle. The cycle is very simple. Trees and plants inhale carbon dioxide (CO_2) and take in water (H_2O) through their roots, which are their umbilical cord to Mother Earth. The sun shines on the leaves and their chlorophyll converts the CO_2. The resultant combination ($H_2O + CO_2$) is 'sugar'. This process is called photosynthesis. In the universal food chain, people and animals then ingest the sugar as food, breathe in oxygen (O_2) and release carbon dioxide and water. Consequently the cycle is in natural balance. Trees, plants and plankton are fostered by the sun and nurtured by the earth. They inhale carbon dioxide and exhale oxygen, whereas people and other living creatures inhale oxygen and exhale carbon dioxide. So the system is held in balance.

The water system is also a natural cycle regulated by the sun and the earth. The sun warms the earth and the sea, from which moisture arises as evaporation, forms clouds and then drops from the sky as rain for daily use. The seashore and the forest thus enjoy the purest air and satisfy the lungs, as well as feeding the other senses, for example with the sweet smell of the earth.

The contrast with the air in the city street could not be more complete, for there the motor car's internal combustion engine emits gases, including carbon monoxide (CO) and carbon dioxode. Through the action of the human lungs, carbon monoxide enters the blood stream and causes death. No wonder people living in poisonous fumes love to escape to the seashore, to the forests and to the mountains. There they can find freedom from the habitual city smells and poisons. There the wind is their breath, the open sky is their mind, the sun is their eye and the seas and the mountains are their whole body. In this heavenly ether, people enjoy the elements, whose nature is to be freely available to all.

The creator in his wisdom also confined the fossil fuels within the body of the earth for this very reason: namely, to maintain the purity of the natural life-cycle. In receiving back into her body the former living organisms, the Law of Conservation of Energy required the rotten remains to be turned back into carboniferous products, the energy store which is vital for life. When carbon is burnt, carbon and oxygen are combined and form carbon dioxide and carbon monoxide. The Degenerate Person in us, in ignorance of the true nature of the earth, rapes her for her fossil fuels and pollutes her fair body with the resultant poisons, and by burning these fuels produces nitrous oxide (N_2O) which is released into the atmosphere, engendering smog. In the worst smog-affected city in the world, Los Angeles, the authorities only measure the smog as carbon monoxide, which is harmful to humans but not the nitrous oxides that damage nature. The Degenerate Person also burns fossil fuels which contain sulphur, which is released as sulphur dioxide. This then mixes with the moisture in the air, and water is thereby added to the sulphur dioxide, producing sulphuric acid (H_2SO_4). This toxic killer then invades the natural water life-cycle and falls as acid rain, destroying the very forests that convert the carbon dioxide and produce the oxygen essential for life on earth. The forests themselves are being cut down at the rate of 40 million acres each year or more than an acre each second, according to the United Nations. The acid rain also penetrates the rivers that nourish the earth and then flow into the sea, thereby destroying the plankton that also produce oxygen, like the trees. Not content with the desecration caused by acid rain, the Degenerate Person even forces the land to higher crop yields by having the audacity to throw fertiliser over her! The excessive use of nitrogen is an act of desecration, for the excess becomes a dangerous pollutant in the water life-cycle.

At the time of the Oil Crisis in 1974, when OPEC raised the price of crude oil by 300% at a stroke, it was estimated that about half the earth's oil-based fossil fuel reserves had been depleted in the previous century and a quarter. The fossilisation process takes millennia. Mankind must clearly seek cleaner energy sources that are renewable and harmless and thereby work within the Law of Conservation of Energy. Yet the power of vested interests has an overpowering need to maintain the status quo, where oil companies dominate the world's economy, governments and banks; where auto companies produce internal combustion engines as a result of massive investments in plant and technology; and where governments derive enormous revenues from both petroleum and vehicles. It will clearly take time, but in the next millennium the Degenerate Person will have exhausted the world supply of fossil fuels – as a practical economic source of energy, that is – and the Creative Person will bring intelligence to bear to identify and develop new energy sources. The technology of 'insolation' will be developed, whereby the sun's exposure to a particular location will be harnessed to produce the cleanest form of natural energy, which is electricity. In fact, the sun radiates the earth with sufficient energy in a single rotation of twenty-four hours to provide enough energy for the world's needs for a whole solar year.

The main problem with electricity is, surprisingly, storage. The biggest storehouse of electricity developed by the super-technological twentieth century still remains the common-or-garden car battery. Creative Person has not been entirely inactive in this vital area and the course of future technological development is clearly in view, and many experimental and production sites are being pioneered. The first practical source for the new energies will therefore undoubtedly be solar energy, as the development of photo-voltaics will economically convert the sun rays directly into electrical energy by means of silicon wafers. Then there is geothermal energy, a completely clean, safe and constant form of energy, which has been used to provide power to city of Genoa since 1906 and is now being actively commercialised in California. In the same state there are several fields of central solar parabolas for concentrating the sun's heat. There are also fields of propellers deriving power from the second main source of the new energies, the wind. Plans are being developed to tap the third source, the sea, by harnessing tides and waves, and by processes such as Ocean Thermal Energy Conversion (OTEC).

Energy can also be stored in the form of hydrogen, which can be derived from water by electrolysis. Solar power has been harnessed in the American space programme to break down water and release oxygen and store hydrogen. Interestingly, a hydrogen car was developed in Montana in 1978, but an American oil major bought the process and no further development was notified. In fact many inventions involving new fuels have been purchased by oil companies, with a conspicuous absence of follow-through research and development. Degenerate Persons inhabit the boardrooms and management offices of oil and chemical majors and industrial process industries; they are found on high intensity farms and in some mass production food-processing and packaging plants; they manufacture 'gas-guzzling' cars and trucks; they are responsible for buses and taxis that take to the road for hire, belching out filthy black fumes as they are not properly serviced.

Mankind's unthinking destruction of the life-force cycle has also extended to the ozone layer, which protects the earth from the sun's harmful ultraviolet (UV) rays. Ozone (O_3) is a molecule made of three oxygen atoms, as opposed to the normal two, and this enables ozone to absorb UV radiation. Chlorine monoxide (ClO) is a chemical by-product of CFCs which are used in air-conditioning and refrigeration, as cleaning solvents in factories and as blowing agents for types of plastic foam, for example in the ubiquitous aerosol spray. Scientists allege that the chlorine atoms from the CFCs attack the ozone layer, which is about sixteen miles above the earth's surface, and take one oxygen atom away, thus forming chlorine monoxide. As the ozone layer breaks up, the sun's UV rays also attack the trees, plants and plankton that drive the life-force cycle, as well as causing serious diseases for humans and animals.

The Degenerate Person, however, is slowly being found out and the Creative Person has awakened to the destruction caused by the Degenerate Person's ignorance and negligence. The Creative Person actually caused world governments to move rapidly to sign the Montreal Protocol in 1987, which called for a 50% reduction in CFC production by 1999, and this process is even being accelerated. Meanwhile the Shell Oil Company is being sued in Texas for more than one billion dollars for allegedly causing widespread effluent seepage. ICI has been accused of polluting many of Britain's rivers with toxic killer chemicals and is being forced to face its neglect and amend its discharge processes. The growth of alternative – meaning 'natural' – farming methods has led to a slump in nitrogen-based fertilisers. ICI was also Britain's largest producer, but after a steady sales decline and mounting losses was forced to sell this whole division to a Finnish company in 1991, at an appropriately low price. Before long, the police will be given powers to arrest any vehicle emitting excess fumes; then the autobus company will not take the risk of fare-paying passengers being held up and of summary roadside fines. The motor-car manufacturers are being given a three-year deadline to fit catalytic converters as standard and to meet exacting emission standards. Mercedes, General Motors and other manufacturers have advanced plans for cleaner electrical cars to be introduced in the 1990s. Major food companies are being taken to court for failure to describe accurately the chemicals and preservatives, some of them harmful, which are required to be disclosed on their product labels.

There is also evidence that the Creative Person is stirring in unexpected quarters, such as in the world's largest pharmaceutical company. At a symposium in New York in January 1991, sponsored by a charity called the Rain Forest Alliance and the New York Botanical Garden's Institute of Economic Botany, a most unusual deal was struck between unlikely partners. A Costa Rican research institute is prospecting for plants, micro-organisms and insects with medicinal properties, which will be screened for use by the giant Merck & Company, which is financially supporting the project. The reason for this unusual attitude is the growing realisation that, with the destruction of the rain forests by logging, by acid rain and by the destruction of the ozone layer, the world is also losing vital plants and organisms that have yielded health cures for centuries. There was no innate understanding of their medicinal use in the so-called developed countries, not least as isolating specific plant compounds is a difficult technical task. The chemical interaction of plant and animal compounds is now understood better and robots can now screen plant compounds round the clock. The Creative Person has woken up to the fact that potentially vital plants for the cure of AIDS, cancer and heart disease are disappearing with the forests at a faster rate than they can be investigated for their medical value.

In the same week that this favourable agreement was announced, Degenerate Person struck back in a most incredible way. In the Umpqua National Park in Oregon there grows a yew tree whose bark yields the drug taxol, a vital substance in the treatment of ovarian cancer, a gift given freely by the earth to mankind. On this occasion, however, Degenerate Man burnt – yes burnt! – a huge pile of downed yew trees. It then transpired that in six of the nine Pacific North West national parks, this precious bark was not even stripped from the yew tree, with a resulting loss of this most precious drug. A director of the National Cancer Institute was quoted in the *New York Times* as saying: 'The supply is finite. In years to come, the needs of taxol will far exceed the supply.' The Institute called this negligent destruction 'shameful and outrageous'. Those who spurn the gifts of the gods often find that the gods do not come to help in their hour of need, for they are only too well versed in the practice of commerce, of giving out freely and in turn receiving sacrifice. The earth is a spirit and is no exception.

There is a clear change of attitude in the governments and peoples of the OECD countries and LDCs, with a growing desire to work in conformity with nature's laws in order to curb desecration of the planet. With the collapse of the USSR and Eastern European economies, however, the full scale of the desecration of the earth behind the former 'Iron Curtain' is being revealed. The evidence is quite appalling. In East Germany the entire country is suffering from pollution from a collapsed industrial infrastructure. Every river carries dangerous levels of toxic waste and the clean-up will take years and cost billions of Deutschemarks. This cost will represent one of the major distortionary factors in the EC's economy in the 1990s and is already causing German monetary supply to expand at over 9%. It is in the former USSR, however, that the true extent of the damage wrought by Degenerate Person is apparent, for pollution has reduced life expectancy to only forty-four years in some cities. The whole vast country is teetering on ecological and economic collapse. Significantly, the ecological condition of the country is one of the biggest economic threats. 'A massive ecological disaster zone threatens' is the way the Russian government's chief adviser on the environment expressed it. Quite apart from the visible evidence of radioactive lakes and sterile land caused by Russian military-industrial activity, there is also the high risk of technogenic emergencies, or invisible disasters waiting to happen. Oil pipeline ruptures and neglect of geological structures under major cities like Moscow are on this hidden agenda.

Mention of Chernobyl, by way of a minor digression, alerts us to the extreme dangers of management and design incompetence in the nuclear industry. The Chernobyl disaster is, unfortunately, seized upon by right-spirited environmentalists as being evidence of the undesirability of nuclear power in general. This stance, however, needs to be examined carefully, for no one would argue that the ubiquitous motor car is environmentally unsound just because there are crashes that kill people, however unpleasant such incidents are for those related to the unfortunate victims. Nuclear power is completely clean and the technology will soon be in place whereby it is entirely self-renewable. True, it produces radioactive waste, but there are perfectly proven ways of handling this waste in an ecologically safe manner. The trouble is that Degenerate Persons have not met their responsibilities to the earth. For example, at Sellafield in Cumbria, in beautiful North-West England, radioactive seepage and waste has polluted the sea, and above-average national levels of cancer are alleged to have been recorded. Nuclear power was the discovery of Einstein, who was an archetypal Creative Person. He formulated that Energy is Mass times the Speed of Light squared ($E = MC^2$), which was the simple and elegant formula that spawned nuclear energy. The French nuclear programme has shown beyond all doubt how effective, clean and safe nuclear energy really is in the hands of competent management, working within the applicable natural and man-made laws.

Meanwhile, under the incompetent management of Soviet Degenerate Person working in a bankrupt system, vast tracts of the Ukraine and Belorussia are uncultivable as a consequence of Chernobyl. Aluminum factories in Uzbekistan produced uncontrolled wastes for years that are now affecting fruit-growing areas. Lakes around Chelyabinsk, in the Urals, the centre of the Soviet nuclear industry, are oozing with plutonium. There is dioxin in mothers' milk in Moscow. The river Volga carries untreated effluent from the South Russian industrial heartland and is slowly killing marine life in the Caspian Sea. The nuclear reactor of the icebreaker ship *Lenin* was abandoned in the Kara Sea. Liquid radioactive waste in storage tanks on the river Techa on the Arctic ocean is overflowing. This desecration of the earth is criminal.

This is all very well, you say, but what has it all got to do with economics?

13. Ecological Postscript

There are two points to be made, one practical and one theoretical. The practical point is that industrialists are looking for new growth industries, to replace declining industries such as defence. The industries that address the problems of pollution in all its forms are set to become one of the growth industries of the near future. These industries will be focused on energy, chemicals, packaging, monitoring, materials, cleansing, food and DNA-based and health specialities manufacture. The theoretical point is more significant. The life-force cycle is a delicate web of nature that is innate to the earth, sun, sea and sky. Creative Man has suddenly awakened to its structure and its implications. There has been a miraculous change of heart right across the world, and while many malpractices continue for the time being unabated, the move is on to outlaw or shame these practices and to work instead within the fragile balance of the eco-system for the good of all mankind, animals and plants. A question poses itself: could the creator of such an intricate and refined ecological system have had no thought for, or made no provision for, an economic system that also reflected a natural balance? It seems unlikely on the evidence; yet all around lies economic chaos, excess and deprivation.

Creative Man in this debate on the environment is addressing the point of interaction between mankind and the eco-system in order to bring the two into harmony, driven by a new appreciation of the natural structure. The task is even widely seen as an urgent one. Now in the realm of economics there is also a need to identify how the two primary factors of production can interact in harmony, based on the inherent structure of the economy. Mankind has found it easier to identify and analyse complex chemical structures, not only on earth but also in the sky and sea, than the British government has to analyse economic realities on earth and manage them within the natural framework. This enquiry from Britain's point of view is just as urgent as the growing movement to protect the earth is for mankind. Just as CFCs must be phased out by 1999, unless new economic thinking and management is in place in Britain for the new millennium, the economy is liable to experience a truly major financial mishap, which could easily cause an otherwise avoidable depression.

Ten Fundamental Principles of Economics

Chapter 1

1. Everything in the man-made world comes from the earth and returns to her.
2. Energy in the living sphere of earth can neither be created nor destroyed, (but $E=MC^2$).
3. The bounty which is given freely by the earth is for distribution to meet the community's needs.
4. The man-made world and everything in it is entirely the result of labour on land, or labour applied to raw materials and substances extracted from beneath its surface.

Chapter 2

5. The earth measures out and regulates economic life with short and long cycles, which are governed by the number 9 and by the sum of 9 raised to the power of 2 plus 9, respectively, as measured in solar years.
6. Those who abuse the earth by failing to observe her laws have to pay the appropriate penalty.

Chapter 3

7. The economic conditions under which labour is applied to land, being the third point, will determine the overall efficiency of an economy.

Chapter 6

8. Increases in property values indirectly create purchasing power beyond production and an asset value that demands more rent from production.
9. The higher property values rise, the more marginal industry becomes. (If

the price of property could be infinite, no industry could afford to pay the rent and everyone would be unemployed.)

Chapter 8

10. The right balance between land and labour can only reach optimum fruition in conditions of free trade.

15

SWOT Analysis of UK plc

Strengths

1 The basic structure for economic recovery (although damaged) is in place:
 • Over 35% of EC's top 500 companies.
 • The City is the EC's largest financial centre.

2 Membership of the EC and the family of English-speaking nations gives the UK an unique two-way perspective for trade and finance.

3 Inherent basic honesty and fairness of the people (although damaged) means that the British people prefer to keep to agreements, pay taxes and respect rules and laws.

4 Morale is down everywhere in the world recession, but British morale is ready to be restored, unlike that of some other countries.

5 Lowest taxes, interest rates (down 47% at 8%) and foreign exchange hurdles in the EC, lowest National Debt in G7 and lowest inflation for many years.

6 The current recession gives the lie to the deception of rising property values, which have damaged the economy ever since the boom-bust cycle that began in the 1960s, and the power of the trade unions has been legally curbed.

Weaknesses

1 Steady decline of the manufacturing sector.

2 Structurally and fiscally not ready to join EMU (even if it wanted to).

3 Corrupt attitudes lead to loss of national determination: 'them and us', 'something for nothing' and A^2LOB^2.

4 Out-of-date management philosophies and organisation still too evident.

5 Central and local government inefficient, expensive and out of fiscal balance.

6 Over-preoccupation with property values and over-supply of credit to this sector.

Opportunities

1 Shift incidence of taxation off industry and on to property values.

2 Attract inward investment from US and Japan (and EC) to target the EC's 320 million consumers (for which EMU is no practical current advantage), and fight for GATT versus CAP.

3 Management renaissance, based on the best characteristics of German and Japanese transplants, particularly communication and co-determination, to be reinforced by defined rules on corporate governance.

4 A government that can identify the real issues and solutions and put things right for the long term and restore confidence, setting an example for the captains of industry and the City to emulate.

5 Fiscal incentives for R&D, investment and training and financial incentives for exports.

6 Curb inflation by targeting the budget strategy to keep property prices and unrestrained pay in check, from the boardroom down.

Threats

1 Lack of leadership in government, commerce and industry:

- Strategic and operational failures.
- Decline of City standards.

2   Failure to capitalise on EC membership by exploiting export opportunities and further attrition in traditional markets, leading to continuation of current account deficit with the EC and in total.

3   Decline of corporate governance, professional standards and levels of service generally.

4   Loss of image of Britain as a reliable manufacturing nation that has become too dependent on service industries, with R & D and training treated as discretionary expenses.

5   Inflation, driven by siren calls to revive the property markets and lack of pay restraint from the boardroom down, is the nation's biggest threat.

6   Failure to regulate money-lending institutions and curb loans to property speculators and owners will create another, entirely avoidable, boom-bust cycle.

Select Bibliography

Cash, William. *Against a Federal Europe*. London: Duckworth, 1991. ISBN: 0-7156-2398-2.

Churchill, Winston Spencer. *The People's Rights*. London: Hodder & Stoughton, 1909. Reprinted by Jonathan Cape, 1970. ISBN: 0-224-61748-6.

Janeway, Eliot. *The Economics of Chaos: On Revitalizing The American Economy*. New York: Truman Talley Books, 1989. ISBN: 0-525-24711-4.

Kondratieff, Nikolai. *The Long Wave Cycle*. New York: Richardson & Snyder, 1984.

Machin, A.J. et al. *Retail Prices, 1914-1990*. London: CSO, 1991. ISBN: 0-11-620499-0.

Maude, The Hon. Francis. *Financial Statement and Budget Report, 1992-93*. London: H.M. Treasury, March 1992.

Newman, K.J. *National Income and Expenditure*, 1979. London: CSO, 1979.

Ruffles, D. *United Kingdom National Accounts, 1991*. London: CSO, 1991. ISBN: 0-11-620452-4.

Schumpeter, Joseph A. *Business Cycles: A Theoretical, Historical, and Statistical Analysis of the Capitalist Process*. New York: McGraw Hill, 1939.

The Land Institute. *Site Value Rating ('The Whitstable Report' 1973)*. London, abridged edition, 1974.

Index

Aerospace, 27, Ul'yanovsk works, 34-35, Farnborough '92, 35, British Aerospace, 36, 66, 69, 93, 111, UAL proposed buy-out, 111-112, British Airways lined up, 112, proposed HLT for AMR/American Airlines, 112, UAL/AMR, 114, 121

Agriculture, 45, values, 76, de-rating, 77, CAP subsidies – see 'CAP', GATT negotiations, 88, 89, 93, 96, 136

America – see 'US'

Banks/Bankers, 23, 24, 28, 29, 35, 41, 62, 63, 69, effect of loans on property prices, 46, 47, 54, 68, industry pays for loan losses, 82, compared to German bankers, 83-84, 106, 108-109, 110, 111, 112, 113, 115, 122, 124, 127, 134, 146-147 1991, lending, 117, banking shake-out due, 134-135, new tax write-off proposals, 146, 147

Bank of England, 40, warnings, 104, nationalisation, 53, 54, 133

Bank of New England, North East corridor property market, 107, 112, 113

Bank of Scotland, 103

Bankrupt Businesses, Seaman Furniture Inc., 71, Lowndes Queensway, 71, Polly Peck, 109, Maxwell Communications, 111, stockbrokers and estate agents, 113-114, Lloyds' Names, 114-115, BCCI, Coloroll, Levitt Group, Maxwell Communications, British & Commonwealth, Mountleigh Properties, Pan-Am, American West, Continental, Wang Computers, Prime Computers, Olympia & York, 116, and the walking wounded including Isosceles, 109, Trump, TWA, GPA Group, Heron Corporation, S&W Berisford, Burton Group, Brent Walkers, Stanhope, Rosehaugh, Regalian, Speyhawk, 116, and Greycoat, 117

Barclays Bank plc, NFC buy-out, 102, 1988 rights issue and lending, 107, GEC bid, 107-108, 1991 lending analysis, 107, 117

British Telecom, 16, 122

Budget, 1991-92 budget, 73-74

Building Societies – see 'Banks/Bankers'

Cadbury Committee, 120, Cadbury Schweppes, 122

Canary Wharf, largest development in Europe, 38, collapses, 113, solution to funding the Jubilee Line, 144

Capital – see 'Investment Capital'

Capital Gains Tax, 75, 84, abolition of, 136

Capitalism, 33-35, profit motive, 34, nature of, 42, 61, 1980s not capitalism, 109-110, needs restructuring, 116

CAP, 55, 88-90, costs average British family £830 p.a., 89, 92, 95-96, 131-132

Car Industry, 16, 26-27, 64, 69, 72, 80, 84, 93, 103, 119, abolition of car tax, 136, 138, future developments, 161

Central Government, 69, 73, receipts and expenditure, 74-75, 125, 135,

140, 145

Churchill, Sir Winston, 98, 155, speech on the 1909 budget, 156-157

Church of England / Church Commissioners, 59

Citicorp, 107

City, the, rents 44, 58, merger mania, 101, 'Big Bang', 102, Cazenove, 103, property values, 113, property stock, 117, integrity of, 119-120

Crime, EC subsidies fraud, 55, black economy, 55-56, gambling, 59, Guinnessgate, 104, fraud, 119, Blue Arrow trial, 120, Lord Roskill's Report, 120, Maxwell scandal, 120

Coal Mining, 25, EC subsidies, 93, 99-100, 110, 122, 158-159

Commonwealth, The, 98, 121, 131

Communism, 31-33, military command economy, 34-35, failings of, 121

Community Charge – see 'Poll Tax'

Commercial Property – see 'Banks/Bankers', 'Land' and 'Leaseholds'

Community Value / Tax, cause of, 38-39, 42, 62, 66, the key, 119, 127, 133, 135, enables abolition of other taxes, 137, 141, key to funding infrastructure, 144, 149, the Bard's warning, 151

Computers, development of, 27, GIGO syndrome, 54-55, Treasury Computer, 50, 71, EC subsidies, 92-93, 114

Confidence, 25, cannot be measured, 52, 117, 134, 141, 148

Conservative Party, 119, 127, 133, 136, 153, and site value rating, 154, 155

Consumers, 25, 40, VAT, 79-80, 89, 93, 115, major engine of recovery, 118-119, 133, 134, 136, 138, 141

Corporation Tax, 78-79, 82, 84,

146-147, 148, 149

Corrupt Attitudes, 51, 'them and us', 58, 'give them an inch and they'll take a mile', 58, 'sod the workers', 59, 'something for nothing', 59, 'I can't take it', 59, 'It's unfair', 60

Corrupt Data, monetary indicators, 50-52, piecework rates, 53-54, GIGO, 54, trade figures, 55, black economy omitted, 56, 130

Council Tax, 73, 81, not a solution, 119

Credit – see 'Banks/Bankers'

Creative Persons, 15, definition of, 16, 18, 23, 26, 27, 30, 33, 57, 59, 65, 69, 89, 95, 102, 108, 109, 110, 121, 133, 151, 159, 160, 161, 162, 164

Cycles – see 'Natural Life Cycles' and 'Economic Cycles'

Debt – see 'Bank/Bankers' and 'PSBR'

Deflation, 46, 64

Degenerate Person(s), 15, definition of, 16, 22, 23, 26, 29, 30, 33, 40, 52, 56, 59, 65, 69, 72, 83, 89, 95, 99, 102-104, 108, 109, 110, Maxwell, 111, 119, 129, 133, 136, 143, 151, 159, 160, 161, 162, 163

Depression, probability of, 24, 26, 41, Great Depression, 20, 22, 24, 77, 83, 88, 164

Devaluation, 11, 60, sterling's decline, 71, form of protectionism, 87, 130, 133

Drexel Burnham, 101, 104, a bridge for fee, 108, goes bust, 112

Earth / Earth Mother, first principle, 14, Russia, 29, 151, 158, 162, 165

Economic Cycles, 19-28, 'Long Wave' theory, 20, Great Cycle, 19, 20, long cycles, 19-25, short cycles, 19, 22, 24, electoral cycles clash, 23, 24, 46, 71, 90, 96-97, 98, 102, 103, 105, 106, 118, 119, 142, 143

Economic Principles, 14-17, 22, 23,

41, 61, 65, 68, 96, 146, 151,
  165-166
Economists, need to know man's
  nature, 15-16, suffer from GIGO
  syndrome, 57
Education, 73, 125, 126, 136, 149
EMU – see 'European Community'
Energy, Law of Conservation of, 14,
  Einstein, 15, North Sea oil, 47, 158,
  Chernobyl, 163
Entrepreneur(s), role in Capitalist
  System, 34, 43, determines rent, 76,
  136-137
ERM – see 'European Community'
European Community, ERM not the
  answer, 69, 88-96, ECU, 90, EMU,
  90, ERM, 90, 91, subsidies, 92-93,
  the 'flamingo factor', 120-121, 131,
  132
Federal Reserve, 53, Federal debt,
  98-99, warnings, 103, 104, 105,
  112, 113
Ferranti plc, 108
France, 12, 22, 72, 83, Napoleon, 84,
  88-89, 92, 95, 131, 132, 133
Free Trade – see 'Protectionism'
GATT – see 'Protectionism' and 'CAP'
General Motors, 16, 64
Germany / Deutschemark, 11, 27-28,
  58, 60, housing, 68-69, 72, 83-84,
  88, 90-91, EC subsidies, 93,
  Allianz, 93, 95, 96, cars, 103, 105,
  114, Deutsche Bank, 122,
  Mitbestimmung, 124,
  Bertriebsverfassungsgesetz, 124,
  133, 134, East German ecological
  desecration, 162
Gross Domestic Product, 41, 118, 126
Hanson Trust plc, 110, 111, 123
Health, 125, 129, 137-138, 152,
  161-162
Houses, not taxed, 39-40, 45, Index,
  57, 62, 1987 values, 76, home

ownership, 83, householders do not
  pay their share of local services,
  85-86, 95, 103, 106, 113, 115, 134,
  myth of values, 134, 135, 138-139,
  145
Income Tax, 55, 75, falls on industry,
  77-79, 84, Thatcher cuts, 100, 126,
  130, 135, 141, 149
Industry, taxes on, 39, 41, relationship
  to land, 42-47, pays payroll taxes,
  77-79, incidence of taxation on,
  81-86, 127, training incentives, 147,
  investment incentives, 149, future
  industries, 164
Inflation, 25, linked to land, 35-36,
  effect on industry, 44-46,
  monetarist approach, 50-52, 57,
  61-65, The Great Inflation, 68, link
  to house prices, 83, 97, 99, 105,
  110, 118, 120, 131, 132, 133, 136
Inheritance Tax, 80, 84, abolition of,
  136
Interest, 34, Muhammad, 34, Russia,
  34, politicians' control of, 53, 63,
  68, 1989 forecast, 71, 76, 92, 99,
  100, 101, 105, 106, 113, 118, 132,
  133, 135, 141, 150
IBM Corporation, 92, 93
Investment Capital, 27, 34, cause of
  shortage of, 44-46, venture capital,
  69, BES, 69, exchange controls, 87,
  90, 92, 93-94, 'transactional'
  capital vs. 'investment' capital,
  109-110, 121-122, investment
  incentives, 141, 144, corporate
  BES, 148, 149
Italy, 11, 12, Luigi and peaches, 55,
  leaves ERM, 95, savings, 95,
  'exclusivity', 95, 123, 130
Japan, 11-12, 28, 47, 58, 88, 92, NEC,
  92-93, Honda, 93, 95, 104, 107,
  109, 112, 113, 118, 123, 141, 168
Joe and Jane, antics at work, 53-54, EC

clones, 55, antics at home, 59-61, Spitfire vs ME109 production, 124, can move home and still afford the beer, 139

Jubilee Line, 38, solution to funding, 144

Juglar, Clement, 22

KKR, RJR-Nabisco HLT, 108-109

Kondratieff, Nikolai, 20, 22

Labour, 14, tribal system, 29-31, communist system, 31-33, capitalist system, 33-41, 46, 65

Labour Party, 152

Lamont, Norman, 11, 52, 56, 57, 97, 96-97, 114, 120

Landlord(s), 44-45, 58, 65, 77, 87, 145

Land, 27, tribal system, 29-31, communist system, 31-33, capitalist system, 33-41, capitalist system creates land value, 35-41, UK values, 41, role in inflation and effect on industry, 41-47, 61, 65, 1987 UK property values, 76, incidence of taxation on, 82-84, 103, surged with inflation, 106, property collapse, 112, 113, 127, fall in values is a long-term blessing, 134

Lawson, Nigel, disastrous 1988 budget, 53, 97, 106, 114

Leasehold(s), 44-45, 64-65, 146

Lenin, 31-32

Lesser Developed Countries, dependent on G7, 23

Liberal Party, 152, 156

Local Government, UK different from Germany, 68-69, 73, 75, funding compared to Europe, 83, effect of business rates, 85-86, 119, education, 125, reform of funding, 135-136, 140, uncontrolled expenditure, 145

Maastricht, Treaty of, 91-92, 131, 132

Major, John, 40, 64, 92, 97, 115, 131, 133, 134, 153

Manufacturing, decline of, 46-47, corrupt data, 53-54, success of Japanese transplants in UK, 58, corrupt attitudes, 58-60, more production cuts inflation, 62, effect of inflation, 64, and of property values increasing, 66-68, value compared to land, 76, effect of taxes on, 77-82, effect of rates on, 85-86, effect of protectionism on, 87, effect of subsidies on, 93, losing self-sustaining mass, 119, compared to Germany, 122-124, how to revive manufacturing, 133-134, need to kill the property myth, 134-135, and cut taxes on production, 136-137, especially employers' contribution, 141-142, work schemes, 143, infrastructure funding, 144, training incentives, 147, corporate venturing proposal, 148, investment incentives, 149, Churchill's solution, 156-157, industries for the future, 164

Marshall Plan, 28

Maxwell, Robert (dec'd), 16, 111, SROs are a farce, 120

MBOs, 69, 71, 101-102, SEC warning, 103, Macy's, 103, RJR-Nabisco, 108-109, Isosceles, 109, 115

Monetarism, 50-53, 62, Friedman's free lunch, 99, 127, 133

Mortgages, the trap, 40, 45, 57, 62, abolish tax relief, 76, compared to Europe, 82-83, 100, double relief, 106, abolition of tax relief, 138, key to trap, 139-140, 144

Natural Life Cycles, 158-162

Oil, 1974 crisis, 27-28, North Sea, 47, OPEC cuts price, 101, mergers, 101, 119, 122, 127, 159

Pay, restraint, 58, effect on property values, 63, Vauxhall Motors, 64, 'take-home pay', 78, pay-roll taxes, 78-79, City salaries, 102

Poll Tax, 73, 81, 84, 119

President Bush, 11, 56, 71, 112, 'no new taxes', 113, 115

President Carter, did not know what he was signing for, 100

President Reagan, 98, 99, cuts taxes, 100, signs Gramm-Rudman-Hollings, 105, prototypical escapee, 115

Production – see 'Manufacturing'

Property – see 'Land'

Protectionism, effect on manufacturing, 87, Fordney-McCumber, 88, Smoot-Hawley, 88, 95-96

PSBR, 57, 74, 99, 118, 126-127, 128, 129, 141, 142, 144

Rates, 65, 73, 81, 84, effect on industry, 85-86, 128, removal of rate support, 140, 145, 149

Recession, 24, 26, 27-28, 29, 53, 57, 69, 96-97, 98-99, 105, 118, 1982-83 recovery, 118

Rent, 34, 44-46, 61, 64-65, economic rent, 67, determination of, 76, definition of, 77, tax on rents 78-79, city rents, 79, 113, 117, 145

Russia (or USSR), 20, patriarchal system, 31-33, privatisation, 33, Ul'yanovsk aerospace works, 34, 61, 66, Gorbachev's 1991 Business Plan, 121, threat and opportunity, 121, ecological desecration, 162-163

Salaries and Wages – see 'Pay'

Savings, basis of capitalism, 33, 40, Italy's savings, 95, already taxed, 136

S&Ls, 100, Milken the crisis, 101, 104, 112

Scargill, Arthur, 25, 99-100

Schumpeter, Joseph, 22

Seattle, Chief, 30-31, 36, 43

Siemens AG, 92, 122

Site Values, explanation of, 37-39, 73, tax on, 81, 128-129, 135

SMEs, provide employment, 69, German model, 124, 148

Social Security, 73, 77-79, 84, 130, abolition of employers' contributions, 141-142, 149

Stock Markets, reflect cycles, 24-25, value compared to property, 76, 98, 'Big Bang', 102-103, SEC warning, 103, booms, 104-105, 'Black Monday', 105-106, 110, 136

Supply and Demand, 34

Takeovers, cross-border restrictions in Europe, 87, 93-94, EC data, 93, merger boom, 101-102, 103, Guinness, 104, the biggest ever, 105, Metsun and GEC, 107-108, RJR-Nabisco, 108-109, Gateway, 109, Morris-Kraft, Time-Warner and TSB-Hill Samuel, 110-111, 112, 123, 147

Target 2000, (Chapter 11), ERM the wrong problem, 131, EC must be a common market, 131, leave Germany to her problems, 132, GATT not CAP, 132, fiscal distortions are the real issue, 132, money supply targets can work with a floating pound, 133, interest rates must be brought down, 133, no need to raise house prices, 134, rather a need to keep property values down by switching incidence of taxation, 134, as interest rates fall, 135, community value tax to raise £25 billion for local government, 135, then abolish car tax, capital gains tax and inheritance tax, 136, and petroleum revenue tax, agricultural levies and stamp duty, 137, increase tax on leaded fuels, tobacco duties and introduce a new carbon tax, 137-138, remove mortgage tax relief and reduce VAT to compensate, 138, plan to nurse house values, 138-139, TIM and TESS' destroy the phantom of the mortgage trap, 139-140, start reducing central government rate support grant to local authorities, 140, eliminate the employers' contribution to social security, 141, spurs inward domestic investment, 141, obtain a return on unemployment, 143, and cut the PSBR, 143, and get on with infrastructure investment, 144, make local government savings, 135, re-establish work ethic, 146, fiscal curbs on bankers' profligacy with property loans, 146-147, boost to SMEs, employment and technology through corporate venturing, 148, investment and training incentives, 149, accept the Bard's advice, 151

Tariffs – see 'Protectionism'

Taxation, 39-40, incidence of, 72-84, fall on industry, 77-79, on wigs and windows, 72, 73-74, 92, the key, 119, 124-127, 128, 132, 134, Single Taxers, 129-130, fiscal change for bank loan provisions, 146-147

Technology, effect on cycles, 25, 26, 27

Tenant(s), 77, 113, 145

Thatcher, Margaret, 59, 73, 81, 97, 98, 99, sees off Scargill, 100, 101, 104, 106, 115, 119, 126-127, 148, 153

Tobacco, 80, 84, 138, 149

Trade Deficits, 47, German policy, 91, UK with EC, 122,

Trade Unions, 45, strikes, 65, 69, 87, 99, miners' strike 1984-85, 99-100, Germany, 124

Transportation, drives cycles, 26-27, Eurotunnel, 38, drives site values, 37-39, 52, Canary Wharf problem, 38-39, and solution, 144, linking to Eurotunnel, 144, Russian submarines, 121, Heathrow, 44, EC railway subsidies, 93, 99, 137

Treasury, HM, 50, 53, 57, 71, 74, 82, 97, 98, 114, 118, 119, 121, 127, 130, 131, 133, 134, 139, 142, 144, 145, 146, 147, 148, 149, 151

Tribal System, 30-32, 36, 43, 61, 116

Trump, Donald, 106, 112, 114

Unemployment, 24, 26, causes of, 46-47, 52, OECD level, 61, causes of, 65-68, 69, SMEs create jobs, 69, in car industry, 72, taxes on employment, 77-79, effect of rates on employment, 85-86, East Germany, 94, Wall Street and City, 113, 118, 130, 136, 141, 142, 143, 148, 149-150

USSR – see 'Russia'

US, 11, site values, 37, leases, 44, 47, 59, black economy, 56, Darman's censorship, 56-59, sales tax, 79-82, British investment in, 87, GATT talks, 89, the 1980s, 98-115, Federal debt, 98, 99, 101, monetary deregulation, 100, 121, 141, 160

Value Added Tax, 39, 55, 79-80, 91-92, 131, 135, 138, 139, 141, 149

Washington, 1992 presidential election, 24, 57-58, freely mixes money with politics, 57, 71, 112

Wasserstein Perella, 109, 112

Whitstable Report 1973, 128-129